THIS JOURNAL
BELONGS TO

_____

_____

_____

THE

100-DAY GOAL

JOURNAL

THE
100-DAY
GOAL
JOURNAL

ACCOMPLISH WHAT MATTERS TO YOU

JOHN LEE DUMAS

STERLING

New York

STERLING
New York

An Imprint of Sterling Publishing Co., Inc.
1166 Avenue of the Americas
New York, NY 10036

ISBN 978-1-4549-3074-7

Distributed in Canada by Sterling Publishing Co., Inc.
c/o Canadian Manda Group, 664 Annette Street
Toronto, Ontario M6S 2C8, Canada
Distributed in the United Kingdom by GMC Distribution Services
Castle Place, 166 High Street, Lewes, East Sussex BN7 1XU, England
Distributed in Australia by NewSouth Books
University of New South Wales, Sydney, NSW 2052, Australia

For information about custom editions, special sales, and premium and
corporate purchases, please contact Sterling Special Sales at 800-805-5489
or specialsales@sterlingpublishing.com.

Manufactured in Singapore

4 6 8 10 9 7 5

sterlingpublishing.com

Interior design by Shannon Nicole Plunkett
Cover design by Igor Satanovsky

A NOTE FROM
THE AUTHOR

What does it take to achieve success? Three things:

1. A clear goal

2. A specific plan to accomplish that goal

3. The discipline to invest the time, energy, and
    effort to execute that plan

What would you like to master? A language? An
instrument? Your health? A business skill? A sport?

No matter what your goal, this journal will guide you
to accomplishing whatever you want over the next 100
days.

All you have to do is trust the process.

John Lee Dumas

THE INSPIRATION BEHIND THIS JOURNAL

In 2012, I was searching for success. I began to study others who had achieved greatness, hoping to uncover the "secret" ingredients that helped them. Entrepreneurs Tim Ferriss and Gary Vaynerchuk became role models for me. They were only a few years older than I was, but they had achieved the type of lifestyle, freedom, and greatness I yearned for. Tim Ferriss's book *The 4-Hour Workweek* revealed how I could better leverage my time and energy. Gary Vaynerchuk's book *Crush It!* showed me the power of hard work, the benefits of focus, and the importance of following one course until reaching success.

These revelations inspired me to launch a daily podcast where I could interview the world's most successful entrepreneurs and ask the questions I needed answered. I called the show *Entrepreneurs on Fire*, and to date, have interviewed more than 2,000 entrepreneurs with the goal of unveiling the path to success.

I did not find the secret ingredients. Instead, I found a list of traits that every successful entrepreneur possessed. It includes the following:

- Courage
- Curiosity
- Persistence
- Work ethic
- A willingness to fail
- A desire to learn from failure
- An insatiable desire for success

Although they're important, these traits will only get you so far. The key I uncovered while studying these 2,000 successful entrepreneurs was the necessity to harness these traits and formulate a clear plan. Without a clear plan, we are all ships without a rudder. We may have the best intentions, but we will be adrift in a sea of distractions and noise.

I created this journal to be your North Star. If you follow the guidance in the following pages, you will establish a clear goal, devise a plan to accomplish that goal, and execute that plan.

HOW THIS
JOURNAL WORKS

Life is busy. *Your* life is busy. If this journal were complicated and time-consuming, it wouldn't work. That's why I created a straightforward process for you to follow, step-by-step and day by day.

Every day, you will use a simple and accessible framework. This framework will guide you toward mastery of your chosen goal.

Every 10 days, you will conduct an evaluation of your progress. This evaluation will provide insights into what is working and what is not. You'll amplify what's been successful and fix what's broken.

By day 100, you will have completed the plan you created and attained your goal.

You are 100 days away from accomplishing your goal. You are 100 days away from achieving success. Day 1 starts today.

ESTABLISH YOUR GOAL

The actual setting of the goal is where most people make their first mistake. Choosing vague goals without setting a timeframe for completion is a common misstep that will make it harder to succeed. You'll have the highest chances of completing your goal if you can answer yes to the following questions.

IS YOUR GOAL CLEAR?

You should be able to easily articulate your goal to another person. It is important to fully understand the task you are taking on.

DOES YOUR GOAL MATTER TO YOU?

To accomplish this goal, it should have a valued impact on your life. If not, you will lose motivation when you're working toward it.

ARE YOU ABLE TO MEASURE THE SUCCESS OF YOUR GOAL WHEN YOU ACHIEVE IT?

The best way to know if you accomplished your goal is by having a way to measure your success, whether it be quantitatively or qualitatively.

DOES YOUR GOAL HAVE AN END DATE?

Your goal must have a specific timeframe it will be accomplished by. Working toward a deadline allows you to establish a plan of action that you can execute over 100 days.

DO YOU HAVE THE TOOLS YOU NEED?

You already have your journal, but you might need to buy additional supplies or find a workspace. For example, if your goal is to train for a 5K in the winter, you might need to purchase warm exercise clothing and look for gyms with treadmills and indoor running tracks.

HAVE YOU THOUGHT ABOUT WHO CAN HELP?

Accomplishing your goal doesn't have to be a solo adventure. Think about the people who will hold you accountable and assist you on your 100-day journey.

DID YOU SET YOUR FIRST TEN-DAY GOAL?

It's important to start off on the right foot, so set a challenging target you will be proud of reaching in the first ten days! (If you're wondering what a ten-day goal is, just read on—I'll explain later!)

To make sure your goal has the attributes that will lead you to success, you'll find a questionnaire on page 18 and sample answers on page 12 to guide you in creating a worthy goal.

FILLING IN YOUR JOURNAL

After you have set your goal, it's time to begin Day 1. This journal is designed to fit into your busy life and ensure you get the most out of every day.

Ten minutes in the morning and five minutes in the evening is all the time you need to dedicate to find success and accomplish your goal.

MORNING

You'll start each day by filling in the Morning page. The prompts here are designed to make sure you stay on top of the tasks that will drive you toward success. You will form powerful habits that will become part of your daily routine. Before long, you will start to thrive on the structure this journal provides and fill every day with meaningful tasks.

EXPRESS YOUR GRATITUDE: If you commit to starting each day by thinking about something you are grateful for, you are intentionally starting your day off on the right foot. It's like getting out of bed each morning on the right side. Yes, it's really that easy!

RESTATE YOUR GOAL: This is important. So many people set a goal and then never think about it. This prompt will ensure you focus on your goal each day. Focus makes the goal grow closer.

SET THREE MICRO-GOALS FOR THE DAY:
These micro-goals will ensure you accomplish meaningful tasks that will keep your momentum going in the right direction. Plus, accomplishing these micro-wins every day is exciting and will keep you motivated as you drive yourself toward your goal.

CREATE AN ACTION PLAN: Now that you know the three micro-goals you need to accomplish, it's time to set an action plan that will ensure you accomplish them. Your action plan helps prioritize your day and consists of individual tasks related to your micro-goal. Your action plan should organize these tasks in order of importance; instead of multitasking, you should accomplish the task at hand before moving onto the next one. There's nothing better than setting up a plan for success every day!

SCHEDULE TIME FOR YOUR TASKS: It is critical to assign start and end times for each task. This will set your mind to its purpose and help you focus during the time you have allotted. Don't overthink the start and end times. Simply write in what you think is needed, and eventrually you will improve at estimating the time it will take to complete each task.

EVENING

At the end of each day, you'll complete the Evening page. This is where you will reflect on what went well and what didn't and ensure your momentum is heading in the right direction. It will soon become an important part of your wind-down routine.

CELEBRATE WINS: All too often we only focus on the bad things that happened over the course of the day. Ensure you recognize and celebrate the great things that happened too.

IDENTIFY THREE STRUGGLES: Every day has its share of struggles, and it's important to identify what might be holding you back.

IDENTIFY THREE SOLUTIONS: Once you've identified three struggles, it's important to find solutions to those problems so that you can improve and resolve any problems moving forward.

EVALUATE YOUR DISCIPLINE AND YOUR OVERALL DAY: Self-evaluation is an important part of the self-improvement process. Give yourself a score to evaluate how well you've stuck to your plan and your overall day. This will allow for honest and open reflection and will also provide an opportunity to visually track your progress over the 100 days. As with to the start and end times, don't overthink this section either. Follow your gut, and you will soon become very adept at accurately scoring yourself.

BUILD YOUR MOMENTUM: Are you closer to your goal at the end of the day than you were at the beginning? If yes, mark it as such so you can see your momentum build. If no, make sure to use the Final Thoughts prompt to work through what the obstacles were.

JOT DOWN YOUR FINAL THOUGHTS: At the end of a productive day, there will be a lot of thoughts swirling around in your head. Get these thoughts out of your head and onto paper. It will be great to reference them at a later date, and it will ensure you get a better night's rest so you can wake up ready to rock another day!

10-DAY REVIEW

Every 10 days, you will be setting and accomplishing a longer-term micro-goal that will get you ten percent closer to your overall goal. For example, if your overall goal is to study a new language and you need to learn 400 vocabulary words, a micro-goal for the next 10 days would be to learn 40 words.

The 10-Day Review sections will hold you accountable to these 10-day goals. You will identify what worked well and what didn't over the course of the past 10 days so you can increase your wins and fix what's not working. Then you'll set your next 10-day goal and be off to the races!

Setting all of these 10-day goals in advance is not advisable because over the course of the 100 days you may fall behind or exceed your expectations. Instead of realigning preexisting 10-day-goals to your current progress, it's easier to set fresh ones every 10 days.

CHECK IN ON YOUR PROGRESS: Did you accomplish your last 10-day micro-goal? If yes, great! Take a minute to be proud of your accomplishment. If no, take a minute to think about why you came up short. There will be more time for reflection later.

IDENTIFY WHAT'S WORKING: Over the last 10 days, you have celebrated many wins. You will choose three that you believe played a big role in your success.

AMPLIFY YOUR WINS: Now that you have identified your top successes, it's time to formulate a plan to turn them into habits.

IDENTIFY WHAT'S NOT WORKING: Just as we have wins, we also have struggles. Identify three consistent or recurring struggles that you faced over the last 10 days. For example, if you are trying to lose weight and have a friend who convinces you to eat ice cream for dessert every night, that's a challenge you must face if you want to accomplish your goal.

ADDRESS YOUR CHALLENGES: Now that you have identified your top struggles, it's time to formulate a plan to minimize the damage they cause. For example, tell your friend that you are not able to be there for ice cream but will show up for a 15-minute after-dinner stroll instead. This way, you are still spending time with your friend, but in a much more productive way that moves you closer to your goal.

CHART YOUR SCORES: At the end of every 10 days, you will record the scores that you've given for your discipline and overall day. The charts provide an opportunity to visually track your progress and motivation over the past 10 days and see trends in your progress as you move forward.

SET YOUR NEXT 10-DAY GOAL: You will find space to establish your next micro-goal. If you accomplished your previous micro-goal, it's time to push the boundaries and make this goal more difficult. If you failed to achieve your previous micro-goal, view this as a fresh opportunity to set a completely new one and over the next ten days implement what you have learned.

REACHING YOUR GOAL

What happens when you reach day 100? It's time to celebrate! You've just accomplished a great feat! Whether you hit the mark or fell short, you have still come a long way. To help you reflect on your experience, there are questions on pages 244–245 that you can answer in as much or as little depth as you desire. The important part is to study your answers and uncover a better understanding of your weaknesses and strengths. This will allow you to continue to improve in every facet of your life.

If you've reached your goal ahead of schedule, congratulations! My recommendation is to extend your goal to a higher level and see what you achieve with the remaining days. If that's not possible, try setting another goal that you can accomplish within the confines of the time you have left. Otherwise, you can skip right to the reflection questions.

MY GOAL

HIT THE GROUND RUNNING AND USE THESE QUESTIONS TO OUTLINE
YOUR GOAL MORE SPECIFICALLY, SET YOUR EXPECTATIONS, AND LIST
ANY RESOURCES THAT WILL HELP ALONG THE WAY.

Describe your goal.

My goal is to write a book about the top ten ways to get a better night's sleep.

Why do you want to accomplish this goal?

I want to be an author as well as an authority figure in the sleep niche. I have the knowledge about the subject, and I know it will help thousands of people if I can get my knowledge down on paper and get the book distributed.

How will you know if you've accomplished this goal?

I will have written a 40,000-word manuscript with an introduction and ten chapters. I will also have an editor and designer who will help me work on the book.

When will you accomplish this goal?

I will accomplish my goal in 100 days.

What are the tools you will use to achieve this goal?

I'll need my computer to work on my manuscript, a timer to keep track of the time I spend on tasks, and this journal to stay on track. I'll also need a quiet place to work.

Who can help you achieve this goal?

I will find an editor and designer who will help me polish

my manuscript. I will also ask family and friends to help

brainstorm ideas or give me feedback if I'm feeling stuck.

NOW THAT YOU'VE ANSWERED THE QUESTIONS ABOVE, RESTATE YOUR GOAL AND MAKE SURE YOU INCLUDE THE DETAILS THAT YOU'VE JUST WRITTEN DOWN.

MY 100-DAY GOAL:

My 100-day goal is to write a 40,000-word book with an

introduction and ten chapters by July 4, about the top

ten ways to get a better night's sleep, so I can share my

knowledge about sleep with thousands of people.

READY TO GET STARTED? WRITE YOUR FIRST TEN-DAY GOAL, AND YOU'RE ON YOUR WAY!

What is your first ten-day goal?

I will make an outline for my book, narrow my list of possible

editors to three, and write 4,000 words.

DAY 1

Date: __January 1st__

MORNING

BEGIN EACH DAY WITH GRATITUDE TO START YOUR DAY ON A
POSITIVE NOTE.

I am grateful for:

__The ability to work on projects I enjoy and find challenging.__

REPEAT YOUR GOAL DAILY TO FOCUS YOUR MIND TO THE TASK AT HAND.

In 99 days, I will:

__Write my very first book.__

ESTABLISH YOUR DAILY MICRO-GOALS AND HOME IN ON WHAT YOU
WANT TO ACCOMPLISH FOR THE DAY.

To achieve this, I will accomplish these three micro-goals today:

1. __I will brainstorm titles and decide on three finalists.__

2. __I will create an outline of the book.__

3. __I will start making a list of potential editors.__

FORMULATING YOUR PLAN FOR THE DAY WILL ENSURE YOU
ACCOMPLISH YOUR MICRO-GOALS.

My action plan for the day:

Task	Start Time	End Time
☑ I will spend an hour perusing books in my genre and write down titles I like.	9:04 am	9:46 am
☑ I will write down twenty possible titles and spend an hour whittling those down to three.	10:14 am	10:57 am
☑ I will research how to create an outline.	11:11 am	11:51 am
☑ I will create the first draft of my book's outline.	12:13 pm	1:01 pm
☑ I will find potential editors who have worked with other writers in my genre.	2:19 pm	3:21 pm

EVENING

Wonderful things that happened today:

I whittled down my potential titles to three. I love them all!

I also created what I would consider a great first-draft

outline.

IDENTIFY WHERE YOU ARE FALLING SHORT SO YOU CAN TAKE
CORRECTIVE ACTION GOING FORWARD.

Three struggles I encountered:

1. I am struggling with the subtitle of my book.

2. Creating an outline is tough!

3. Finding an editor in my genre and price range is going to be hard!

AFTER YOU IDENTIFY YOUR STRUGGLES, ESTABLISH A PLAN TO SOLVE THEM.

Possible solutions for these struggles:

1. I'll survey my friends and family for subtitles ideas.

2. I'll find an experienced author to work with me on the second draft.

3. I'll ask authors to recommend editors who might be a good fit.

HOW WELL DID YOU STICK TO YOUR ACTION PLAN? GIVE A RATING OF
1 FOR NOT AT ALL AND 5 FOR PERFECTLY. GIVE A RATING OF 1 FOR A
HORRIBLE DAY AND 5 FOR A PERFECT DAY.

DISCIPLINE: 1 2 ③ 4 5   *OVERALL DAY:* 1 ② 3 4 5

HOLD YOURSELF ACCOUNTABLE FOR THE PROGRESS YOU'VE MADE.

Am I closer to my goal today than I was yesterday?

☑ Yes   ☐ No

WE RARELY GIVE OURSELVES TIME AND SPACE JUST TO THINK. TAKE
YOUR TIME, REFLECT ON THE DAY, AND WRITE DOWN THE THOUGHTS
AS THEY COME.

Final thought of the day:

I uncovered some serious things I need to work on, but I look

forward to learning more!

10-DAY REVIEW

Did I accomplish my ten-day goal?

☑ Yes   ☐ No

Three things that worked well over the last 10 days:

1. Having two 1-hour time blocks of focused writing time.

2. Talking with successful self-published authors. I learned so much!

3. Surveying my friends and family. They have great ideas!

My plan to amplify these wins:

1. I will commit to at least two 1-hour writing blocks every day.

2. I want to have one 20-minute chat with an author each Friday.

3. I will study the marketing strategies of successful authors.

Three things that I struggled with over the last 10 days:

1. Getting responses from authors. They all seem so busy!

2. Coming up with marketing plans for my book's launch.

3. Staying distraction-free.

My plan to fix these struggles:

1. I will double down on my outreach and find authors to mentor me.

2. I will talk to successful self-published authors about marketing.

3. My smartphone is going into airplane mode. Simple as that.

CHART YOUR DAILY DISCIPLINE AND OVERALL DAY SCORES AND SEE
HOW THEY HAVE FLUCTUATED IN THE PAST TEN DAYS.

DISCIPLINE CHART

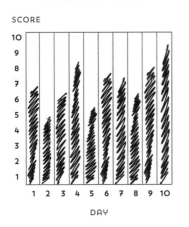

SCORE

DAY

OVERALL DAY CHART

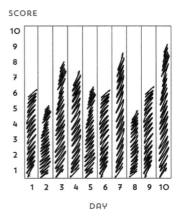

SCORE

DAY

WRITE DOWN YOUR NEXT TEN-DAY GOAL. MAKE IT AN OBJECTIVE
THAT WILL BRING YOU AT LEAST TEN PERCENT CLOSER TO YOUR
OVERALL GOAL.

MY NEXT TEN-DAY GOAL:

I will have 8,000 words written!

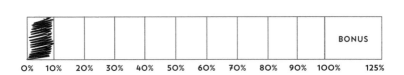

0% 10% 20% 30% 40% 50% 60% 70% 80% 90% 100% 125%

BONUS

MY GOAL

Describe your goal.

_____

_____

_____

_____

Why do you want to accomplish this goal?

_____

_____

_____

_____

How will you know if you've accomplished this goal?

_____

_____

_____

_____

When will you accomplish this goal?

_____

_____

_____

_____

What are the tools you will use to achieve this goal?

_____

_____

_____

_____

Who can help you achieve this goal?

_____

_____

_____

_____

MY 100-DAY GOAL:

_____

_____

_____

_____

What is your first ten-day goal?

_____

_____

_____

_____

"IF ONE ADVANCES CONFIDENTLY IN THE
DIRECTION OF HIS DREAMS, AND ENDEAVORS
TO LIVE THE LIFE WHICH HE HAS IMAGINED,
HE WILL MEET WITH A SUCCESS UNEXPECTED
IN COMMON HOURS."

—Henry David Thoreau, *Walden*

CALENDAR

DAY 1	DAY 2	DAY 3	DAY 4	DAY 5
DATE:	DATE:	DATE:	DATE:	DATE:
DAY 6	**DAY 7**	**DAY 8**	**DAY 9**	**DAY 10**
DATE:	DATE:	DATE:	DATE:	DATE: **10-DAY REVIEW**
DAY 11	DAY 12	DAY 13	DAY 14	DAY 15
DATE:	DATE:	DATE:	DATE:	DATE:
DAY 16	**DAY 17**	**DAY 18**	**DAY 19**	**DAY 20**
DATE:	DATE:	DATE:	DATE:	DATE: **10-DAY REVIEW**
DAY 21	DAY 22	DAY 23	DAY 24	DAY 25
DATE:	DATE:	DATE:	DATE:	DATE:

DAY 26 DATE:	DAY 27 DATE:	DAY 28 DATE:	DAY 29 DATE:	DAY 30 DATE: 10-DAY REVIEW
DAY 31 DATE:	DAY 32 DATE:	DAY 33 DATE:	DAY 34 DATE:	DAY 35 DATE:
DAY 36 DATE:	DAY 37 DATE:	DAY 38 DATE:	DAY 39 DATE:	DAY 40 DATE: 10-DAY REVIEW
DAY 41 DATE:	DAY 42 DATE:	DAY 43 DATE:	DAY 44 DATE:	DAY 45 DATE:
DAY 46 DATE:	DAY 47 DATE:	DAY 48 DATE:	DAY 49 DATE:	DAY 50 DATE: 10-DAY REVIEW

DAY 51	DAY 52	DAY 53	DAY 54	DAY 55
DATE:	DATE:	DATE:	DATE:	DATE:
DAY 56	DAY 57	DAY 58	DAY 59	DAY 60
DATE:	DATE:	DATE:	DATE:	DATE:
				10-DAY REVIEW
DAY 61	DAY 62	DAY 63	DAY 64	DAY 65
DATE:	DATE:	DATE:	DATE:	DATE:
DAY 66	DAY 67	DAY 68	DAY 69	DAY 70
DATE:	DATE:	DATE:	DATE:	DATE:
				10-DAY REVIEW
DAY 71	DAY 72	DAY 73	DAY 74	DAY 75
DATE:	DATE:	DATE:	DATE:	DATE:

DAY 76	DAY 77	DAY 78	DAY 79	DAY 80
DATE:	DATE:	DATE:	DATE:	DATE:
				10-DAY REVIEW
DAY 81	DAY 82	DAY 83	DAY 84	DAY 85
DATE:	DATE:	DATE:	DATE:	DATE:
DAY 86	DAY 87	DAY 88	DAY 89	DAY 90
DATE:	DATE:	DATE:	DATE:	DATE:
				10-DAY REVIEW
DAY 91	DAY 92	DAY 93	DAY 94	DAY 95
DATE:	DATE:	DATE:	DATE:	DATE:
DAY 96	DAY 97	DAY 98	DAY 99	DAY 100
DATE:	DATE:	DATE:	DATE:	DATE:
				10-DAY REVIEW

DAY 1

Date: _____

I am grateful for:

_____

_____

In 99 days, I will:

_____

_____

To achieve this, I will accomplish these three micro-goals today:

1. _____

2. _____

3. _____

My action plan for the day:

Task	Start Time	End Time
☐		
☐		
☐		
☐		
☐		

EVENING

Wonderful things that happened today:

_____

_____

_____

Three struggles I encountered:

1. _____

2. _____

3. _____

Possible solutions for these struggles:

1. _____

2. _____

3. _____

DISCIPLINE: 1 2 3 4 5   OVERALL DAY: 1 2 3 4 5

Am I closer to my goal today than I was yesterday?

☐ Yes   ☐ No

Final thought of the day:

_____

_____

_____

_____

_____

DAY 2

Date: _____

MORNING

I am grateful for:

_____

_____

In 98 days, I will:

_____

_____

To achieve this, I will accomplish these three micro-goals today:

1. _____

2. _____

3. _____

My action plan for the day:

Task	Start Time	End Time
☐		
☐		
☐		
☐		
☐		

Wonderful things that happened today:

_____

_____

_____

Three struggles I encountered:

1. _____

2. _____

3. _____

Possible solutions for these struggles:

1. _____

2. _____

3. _____

DISCIPLINE: 1 2 3 4 5 *OVERALL DAY:* 1 2 3 4 5

Am I closer to my goal today than I was yesterday?

☐ Yes   ☐ No

Final thought of the day:

_____

_____

_____

_____

_____

DAY 3

Date: _____

I am grateful for:

_____

_____

In 97 days, I will:

_____

_____

To achieve this, I will accomplish these three micro-goals today:

1. _____

2. _____

3. _____

My action plan for the day:

Task	Start Time	End Time
☐		
☐		
☐		
☐		
☐		

EVENING

Wonderful things that happened today:

_____

_____

_____

Three struggles I encountered:

1. _____

2. _____

3. _____

Possible solutions for these struggles:

1. _____

2. _____

3. _____

DISCIPLINE: 1   2   3   4   5   OVERALL DAY: 1   2   3   4   5

Am I closer to my goal today than I was yesterday?

☐ Yes   ☐ No

Final thought of the day:

_____

_____

_____

_____

_____

DAY 4

Date: _____

MORNING

I am grateful for:

_____

_____

In 96 days, I will:

_____

_____

To achieve this, I will accomplish these three micro-goals today:

1. _____

2. _____

3. _____

My action plan for the day:

Task	Start Time	End Time
☐		
☐		
☐		
☐		
☐		

EVENING

Wonderful things that happened today:

_____

_____

_____

Three struggles I encountered:

1. _____

2. _____

3. _____

Possible solutions for these struggles:

1. _____

2. _____

3. _____

DISCIPLINE: 1 2 3 4 5   OVERALL DAY: 1 2 3 4 5

Am I closer to my goal today than I was yesterday?

☐ Yes   ☐ No

Final thought of the day:

_____

_____

_____

_____

_____

DAY 5

Date: _____

MORNING

I am grateful for:

_____

_____

In 95 days, I will:

_____

_____

To achieve this, I will accomplish these three micro-goals today:

1. _____

2. _____

3. _____

My action plan for the day:

Task	Start Time	End Time
☐		
☐		
☐		
☐		
☐		

EVENING

Wonderful things that happened today:

_____

_____

_____

Three struggles I encountered:

1. _____

2. _____

3. _____

Possible solutions for these struggles:

1. _____

2. _____

3. _____

DISCIPLINE: 1 2 3 4 5   OVERALL DAY: 1 2 3 4 5

Am I closer to my goal today than I was yesterday?

☐ Yes   ☐ No

Final thought of the day:

_____

_____

_____

_____

_____

DAY 6

Date: _____

MORNING

I am grateful for:

_____

_____

In 94 days, I will:

_____

_____

To achieve this, I will accomplish these three micro-goals today:

1. _____

2. _____

3. _____

My action plan for the day:

Task	Start Time	End Time
☐		
☐		
☐		
☐		
☐		

Wonderful things that happened today:

_____

_____

_____

Three struggles I encountered:

1. _____

2. _____

3. _____

Possible solutions for these struggles:

1. _____

2. _____

3. _____

DISCIPLINE: 1 2 3 4 5   OVERALL DAY: 1 2 3 4 5

Am I closer to my goal today than I was yesterday?

☐ Yes   ☐ No

Final thought of the day:

_____

_____

_____

_____

_____

DAY 7

Date: _____

MORNING

I am grateful for:

_____

_____

In 93 days, I will:

_____

_____

To achieve this, I will accomplish these three micro-goals today:

1. _____

2. _____

3. _____

My action plan for the day:

Task	Start Time	End Time
☐		
☐		
☐		
☐		
☐		

EVENING

Wonderful things that happened today:

_____

_____

_____

Three struggles I encountered:

1. _____

2. _____

3. _____

Possible solutions for these struggles:

1. _____

2. _____

3. _____

DISCIPLINE: 1 2 3 4 5   OVERALL DAY: 1 2 3 4 5

Am I closer to my goal today than I was yesterday?

☐ Yes   ☐ No

Final thought of the day:

_____

_____

_____

_____

_____

DAY 8

Date: _____

MORNING

I am grateful for:

_____

_____

In 92 days, I will:

_____

_____

To achieve this, I will accomplish these three micro-goals today:

1. _____

2. _____

3. _____

My action plan for the day:

Task	Start Time	End Time
☐		
☐		
☐		
☐		
☐		

EVENING

Wonderful things that happened today:

_____

_____

_____

Three struggles I encountered:

1. _____

2. _____

3. _____

Possible solutions for these struggles:

1. _____

2. _____

3. _____

DISCIPLINE: 1 2 3 4 5   OVERALL DAY: 1 2 3 4 5

Am I closer to my goal today than I was yesterday?

☐ Yes   ☐ No

Final thought of the day:

_____

_____

_____

_____

_____

DAY 9

Date: _____

MORNING

I am grateful for:

_____

_____

In 91 days, I will:

_____

_____

To achieve this, I will accomplish these three micro-goals today:

1. _____

2. _____

3. _____

My action plan for the day:

Task	Start Time	End Time
☐		
☐		
☐		
☐		
☐		

EVENING

Wonderful things that happened today:

_____

_____

_____

Three struggles I encountered:

1. _____

2. _____

3. _____

Possible solutions for these struggles:

1. _____

2. _____

3. _____

DISCIPLINE: 1 2 3 4 5   OVERALL DAY: 1 2 3 4 5

Am I closer to my goal today than I was yesterday?

☐ Yes   ☐ No

Final thought of the day:

_____

_____

_____

_____

_____

DAY 10

MORNING

I am grateful for:

_____

_____

In 90 days, I will:

_____

_____

To achieve this, I will accomplish these three micro-goals today:

1. _____

2. _____

3. _____

My action plan for the day:

Task	Start Time	End Time
☐		
☐		
☐		
☐		
☐		

EVENING

Wonderful things that happened today:

_____

_____

_____

Three struggles I encountered:

1. _____

2. _____

3. _____

Possible solutions for these struggles:

1. _____

2. _____

3. _____

DISCIPLINE: 1 2 3 4 5   OVERALL DAY: 1 2 3 4 5

Am I closer to my goal today than I was yesterday?

☐ Yes   ☐ No

Final thought of the day:

_____

_____

_____

_____

_____

10-DAY REVIEW

Did I accomplish my 10-day goal?

☐ Yes ☐ No

Three things that worked well over the last 10 days:

1. _____

2. _____

3. _____

My plan to amplify these wins:

1. _____

2. _____

3. _____

Three things that I struggled with over the last 10 days:

1. _____

2. _____

3. _____

My plan to fix these struggles:

1. _____

2. _____

3. _____

DISCIPLINE CHART

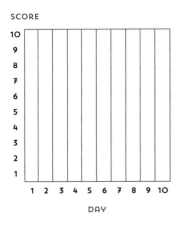

OVERALL DAY CHART

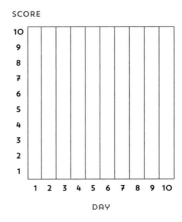

MY NEXT 10-DAY GOAL:

_____

_____

_____

_____

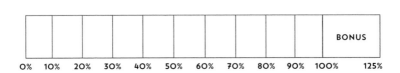

> "TO ACCOMPLISH GREAT THINGS
> WE MUST NOT ONLY ACT, BUT ALSO DREAM;
> NOT ONLY PLAN, BUT ALSO BELIEVE."
>
> —Anatole France

DAY 11

Date: _____

MORNING

I am grateful for:

_____

_____

In 89 days, I will:

_____

_____

To achieve this, I will accomplish these three micro-goals today:

1. _____

2. _____

3. _____

My action plan for the day:

Task	Start Time	End Time
☐		
☐		
☐		
☐		
☐		

EVENING

Wonderful things that happened today:

_____

_____

_____

Three struggles I encountered:

1. _____

2. _____

3. _____

Possible solutions for these struggles:

1. _____

2. _____

3. _____

DISCIPLINE: 1 2 3 4 5   OVERALL DAY: 1 2 3 4 5

Am I closer to my goal today than I was yesterday?

☐ Yes   ☐ No

Final thought of the day:

_____

_____

_____

_____

_____

DAY 12

MORNING

I am grateful for:

_____

_____

In 88 days, I will:

_____

_____

To achieve this, I will accomplish these three micro-goals today:

1. _____

2. _____

3. _____

My action plan for the day:

Task	Start Time	End Time
☐		
☐		
☐		
☐		
☐		

EVENING

Wonderful things that happened today:

_____

_____

_____

Three struggles I encountered:

1. _____

2. _____

3. _____

Possible solutions for these struggles:

1. _____

2. _____

3. _____

DISCIPLINE: 1 2 3 4 5   *OVERALL DAY:* 1 2 3 4 5

Am I closer to my goal today than I was yesterday?

☐ Yes   ☐ No

Final thought of the day:

_____

_____

_____

_____

_____

DAY 13

Date: _____

MORNING

I am grateful for:

_____

_____

In 87 days, I will:

_____

_____

To achieve this, I will accomplish these three micro-goals today:

1. _____

2. _____

3. _____

My action plan for the day:

Task	Start Time	End Time
☐		
☐		
☐		
☐		
☐		

EVENING

Wonderful things that happened today:

_____

_____

_____

Three struggles I encountered:

1. _____

2. _____

3. _____

Possible solutions for these struggles:

1. _____

2. _____

3. _____

DISCIPLINE: 1 2 3 4 5   OVERALL DAY: 1 2 3 4 5

Am I closer to my goal today than I was yesterday?

☐ Yes   ☐ No

Final thought of the day:

_____

_____

_____

_____

_____

DAY 14

Date: _____

MORNING

I am grateful for:

_____

_____

In 86 days, I will:

_____

_____

To achieve this, I will accomplish these three micro-goals today:

1. _____

2. _____

3. _____

My action plan for the day:

Task	Start Time	End Time
☐		
☐		
☐		
☐		
☐		

Wonderful things that happened today:

_____

_____

_____

Three struggles I encountered:

1. _____

2. _____

3. _____

Possible solutions for these struggles:

1. _____

2. _____

3. _____

DISCIPLINE: 1 2 3 4 5 OVERALL DAY: 1 2 3 4 5

Am I closer to my goal today than I was yesterday?

☐ Yes   ☐ No

Final thought of the day:

_____

_____

_____

_____

_____

DAY 15

Date: _____

I am grateful for:

_____

_____

In 85 days, I will:

_____

_____

To achieve this, I will accomplish these three micro-goals today:

1. _____

2. _____

3. _____

My action plan for the day:

Task	Start Time	End Time
☐		
☐		
☐		
☐		
☐		

EVENING

Wonderful things that happened today:

_____

_____

_____

Three struggles I encountered:

1. _____

2. _____

3. _____

Possible solutions for these struggles:

1. _____

2. _____

3. _____

DISCIPLINE: 1 2 3 4 5   OVERALL DAY: 1 2 3 4 5

Am I closer to my goal today than I was yesterday?

☐ Yes   ☐ No

Final thought of the day:

_____

_____

_____

_____

_____

DAY 16

Date: _____

MORNING

I am grateful for:

_____

_____

In 84 days, I will:

_____

_____

To achieve this, I will accomplish these three micro-goals today:

1. _____

2. _____

3. _____

My action plan for the day:

Task	Start Time	End Time
☐		
☐		
☐		
☐		
☐		

EVENING

Wonderful things that happened today:

_____

_____

_____

Three struggles I encountered:

1. _____

2. _____

3. _____

Possible solutions for these struggles:

1. _____

2. _____

3. _____

DISCIPLINE: 1 2 3 4 5   OVERALL DAY: 1 2 3 4 5

Am I closer to my goal today than I was yesterday?

☐ Yes   ☐ No

Final thought of the day:

_____

_____

_____

_____

_____

DAY 17

Date: _____

MORNING

I am grateful for:

_____

_____

In 83 days, I will:

_____

_____

To achieve this, I will accomplish these three micro-goals today:

1. _____

2. _____

3. _____

My action plan for the day:

Task	Start Time	End Time
☐		
☐		
☐		
☐		
☐		

EVENING

Wonderful things that happened today:

_____

_____

_____

Three struggles I encountered:

1. _____

2. _____

3. _____

Possible solutions for these struggles:

1. _____

2. _____

3. _____

DISCIPLINE: 1 2 3 4 5   OVERALL DAY: 1 2 3 4 5

Am I closer to my goal today than I was yesterday?

☐ Yes   ☐ No

Final thought of the day:

_____

_____

_____

_____

_____

DAY 18

Date: _____

I am grateful for:

_____

_____

In 82 days, I will:

_____

_____

To achieve this, I will accomplish these three micro-goals today:

1. _____

2. _____

3. _____

My action plan for the day:

Task	Start Time	End Time
☐		
☐		
☐		
☐		
☐		

EVENING

Wonderful things that happened today:

_____

_____

_____

Three struggles I encountered:

1. _____

2. _____

3. _____

Possible solutions for these struggles:

1. _____

2. _____

3. _____

DISCIPLINE: 1 2 3 4 5   OVERALL DAY: 1 2 3 4 5

Am I closer to my goal today than I was yesterday?

☐ Yes   ☐ No

Final thought of the day:

_____

_____

_____

_____

_____

DAY 19

Date: _____

MORNING

I am grateful for:

_____

_____

In 81 days, I will:

_____

_____

To achieve this, I will accomplish these three micro-goals today:

1. _____

2. _____

3. _____

My action plan for the day:

Task	Start Time	End Time
☐		
☐		
☐		
☐		
☐		

EVENING

Wonderful things that happened today:

_____

_____

_____

Three struggles I encountered:

1. _____

2. _____

3. _____

Possible solutions for these struggles:

1. _____

2. _____

3. _____

DISCIPLINE: 1 2 3 4 5   OVERALL DAY: 1 2 3 4 5

Am I closer to my goal today than I was yesterday?

☐ Yes   ☐ No

Final thought of the day:

_____

_____

_____

_____

_____

DAY 20

Date: _____

MORNING

I am grateful for:

_____

_____

In 80 days, I will:

_____

_____

To achieve this, I will accomplish these three micro-goals today:

1. _____

2. _____

3. _____

My action plan for the day:

Task	Start Time	End Time
☐		
☐		
☐		
☐		
☐		

EVENING

Wonderful things that happened today:

_____

_____

_____

Three struggles I encountered:

1. _____

2. _____

3. _____

Possible solutions for these struggles:

1. _____

2. _____

3. _____

DISCIPLINE: 1 2 3 4 5   OVERALL DAY: 1 2 3 4 5

Am I closer to my goal today than I was yesterday?

☐ Yes   ☐ No

Final thought of the day:

_____

_____

_____

_____

_____

10-DAY REVIEW

Did I accomplish my 10-day goal?

☐ Yes ☐ No

Three things that worked well over the last 10 days:

1. _____

2. _____

3. _____

My plan to amplify these wins:

1. _____

2. _____

3. _____

Three things that I struggled with over the last 10 days:

1. _____

2. _____

3. _____

My plan to fix these struggles:

1. _____

2. _____

3. _____

DISCIPLINE CHART

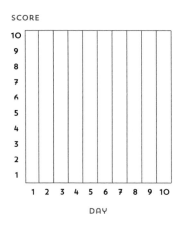

OVERALL DAY CHART

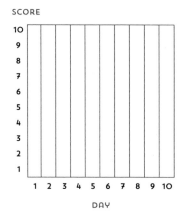

MY NEXT 10-DAY GOAL:

_____

_____

_____

_____

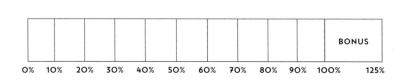

"DETERMINE THAT THE THING CAN
AND SHALL BE DONE, AND THEN WE
SHALL FIND THE WAY."

—Abraham Lincoln

DAY 21

Date: _____

I am grateful for:

_____

_____

In 79 days, I will:

_____

_____

To achieve this, I will accomplish these three micro-goals today:

1. _____

2. _____

3. _____

My action plan for the day:

Task	Start Time	End Time
☐		
☐		
☐		
☐		
☐		

EVENING

Wonderful things that happened today:

_____

_____

_____

Three struggles I encountered:

1. _____

2. _____

3. _____

Possible solutions for these struggles:

1. _____

2. _____

3. _____

DISCIPLINE: 1 2 3 4 5   OVERALL DAY: 1 2 3 4 5

Am I closer to my goal today than I was yesterday?

☐ Yes   ☐ No

Final thought of the day:

_____

_____

_____

_____

_____

DAY 22

Date: _____

MORNING

I am grateful for:

_____

_____

In 78 days, I will:

_____

_____

To achieve this, I will accomplish these three micro-goals today:

1. _____

2. _____

3. _____

My action plan for the day:

Task	Start Time	End Time
☐		
☐		
☐		
☐		
☐		

EVENING

Wonderful things that happened today:

_____

_____

_____

Three struggles I encountered:

1. _____

2. _____

3. _____

Possible solutions for these struggles:

1. _____

2. _____

3. _____

DISCIPLINE: 1 2 3 4 5 OVERALL DAY: 1 2 3 4 5

Am I closer to my goal today than I was yesterday?

☐ Yes   ☐ No

Final thought of the day:

_____

_____

_____

_____

_____

DAY 23

Date: _____

I am grateful for:

_____

_____

In 77 days, I will:

_____

_____

To achieve this, I will accomplish these three micro-goals today:

1. _____

2. _____

3. _____

My action plan for the day:

Task	Start Time	End Time
☐		
☐		
☐		
☐		
☐		

EVENING

Wonderful things that happened today:

_____

_____

_____

Three struggles I encountered:

1. _____

2. _____

3. _____

Possible solutions for these struggles:

1. _____

2. _____

3. _____

DISCIPLINE: 1 2 3 4 5   OVERALL DAY: 1 2 3 4 5

Am I closer to my goal today than I was yesterday?

☐ Yes   ☐ No

Final thought of the day:

_____

_____

_____

_____

_____

DAY 24

Date: _____

MORNING

I am grateful for:

_____

_____

In 76 days, I will:

_____

_____

To achieve this, I will accomplish these three micro-goals today:

1. _____

2. _____

3. _____

My action plan for the day:

Task	Start Time	End Time
☐		
☐		
☐		
☐		
☐		

EVENING

Wonderful things that happened today:

_____

_____

_____

Three struggles I encountered:

1. _____

2. _____

3. _____

Possible solutions for these struggles:

1. _____

2. _____

3. _____

DISCIPLINE: 1 2 3 4 5   OVERALL DAY: 1 2 3 4 5

Am I closer to my goal today than I was yesterday?

☐ Yes   ☐ No

Final thought of the day:

_____

_____

_____

_____

_____

DAY 25

Date: _____

MORNING

I am grateful for:

_____

_____

In 75 days, I will:

_____

_____

To achieve this, I will accomplish these three micro-goals today:

1. _____

2. _____

3. _____

My action plan for the day:

Task	Start Time	End Time
☐		
☐		
☐		
☐		
☐		

EVENING

Wonderful things that happened today:

_____

_____

_____

Three struggles I encountered:

1. _____

2. _____

3. _____

Possible solutions for these struggles:

1. _____

2. _____

3. _____

DISCIPLINE: 1 2 3 4 5   OVERALL DAY: 1 2 3 4 5

Am I closer to my goal today than I was yesterday?

☐ Yes   ☐ No

Final thought of the day:

_____

_____

_____

_____

_____

DAY 26

Date: _____

I am grateful for:

_____

_____

In 74 days, I will:

_____

_____

To achieve this, I will accomplish these three micro-goals today:

1. _____

2. _____

3. _____

My action plan for the day:

Task	Start Time	End Time
☐		
☐		
☐		
☐		
☐		

EVENING

Wonderful things that happened today:

_____

_____

_____

Three struggles I encountered:

1. _____

2. _____

3. _____

Possible solutions for these struggles:

1. _____

2. _____

3. _____

DISCIPLINE: 1 2 3 4 5   OVERALL DAY: 1 2 3 4 5

Am I closer to my goal today than I was yesterday?

☐ Yes   ☐ No

Final thought of the day:

_____

_____

_____

_____

_____

DAY 27

Date: _____

I am grateful for:

_____

_____

In 73 days, I will:

_____

_____

To achieve this, I will accomplish these three micro-goals today:

1. _____

2. _____

3. _____

My action plan for the day:

Task	Start Time	End Time
☐		
☐		
☐		
☐		
☐		

EVENING

Wonderful things that happened today:

_____

_____

_____

Three struggles I encountered:

1. _____

2. _____

3. _____

Possible solutions for these struggles:

1. _____

2. _____

3. _____

DISCIPLINE: 1 2 3 4 5   OVERALL DAY: 1 2 3 4 5

Am I closer to my goal today than I was yesterday?

☐ Yes   ☐ No

Final thought of the day:

_____

_____

_____

_____

_____

DAY 28

MORNING

I am grateful for:

_____

_____

In 72 days, I will:

_____

_____

To achieve this, I will accomplish these three micro-goals today:

1. _____

2. _____

3. _____

My action plan for the day:

Task	Start Time	End Time
☐		
☐		
☐		
☐		
☐		

EVENING

Wonderful things that happened today:

_____

_____

_____

Three struggles I encountered:

1. _____

2. _____

3. _____

Possible solutions for these struggles:

1. _____

2. _____

3. _____

DISCIPLINE: 1 2 3 4 5   OVERALL DAY: 1 2 3 4 5

Am I closer to my goal today than I was yesterday?

☐ Yes   ☐ No

Final thought of the day:

_____

_____

_____

_____

_____

DAY 29

MORNING

I am grateful for:

_____

_____

In 71 days, I will:

_____

_____

To achieve this, I will accomplish these three micro-goals today:

1. _____

2. _____

3. _____

My action plan for the day:

Task	Start Time	End Time
☐		
☐		
☐		
☐		
☐		

EVENING

Wonderful things that happened today:

_____

_____

_____

Three struggles I encountered:

1. _____

2. _____

3. _____

Possible solutions for these struggles:

1. _____

2. _____

3. _____

DISCIPLINE: 1 2 3 4 5   OVERALL DAY: 1 2 3 4 5

Am I closer to my goal today than I was yesterday?

☐ Yes   ☐ No

Final thought of the day:

_____

_____

_____

_____

_____

DAY 30

Date: _____

I am grateful for:

_____

_____

In 70 days, I will:

_____

_____

To achieve this, I will accomplish these three micro-goals today:

1. _____

2. _____

3. _____

My action plan for the day:

Task	Start Time	End Time
☐		
☐		
☐		
☐		
☐		

EVENING

Wonderful things that happened today:

_____

_____

_____

Three struggles I encountered:

1. _____

2. _____

3. _____

Possible solutions for these struggles:

1. _____

2. _____

3. _____

DISCIPLINE: 1 2 3 4 5   OVERALL DAY: 1 2 3 4 5

Am I closer to my goal today than I was yesterday?

☐ Yes   ☐ No

Final thought of the day:

_____

_____

_____

_____

_____

10-DAY REVIEW

Did I accomplish my 10-day goal?

☐ Yes ☐ No

Three things that worked well over the last 10 days:

1. _____
2. _____
3. _____

My plan to amplify these wins:

1. _____
2. _____
3. _____

Three things that I struggled with over the last 10 days:

1. _____
2. _____
3. _____

My plan to fix these struggles:

1. _____
2. _____
3. _____

DISCIPLINE CHART

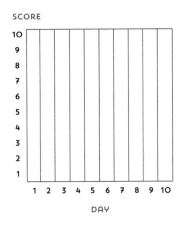

OVERALL DAY CHART

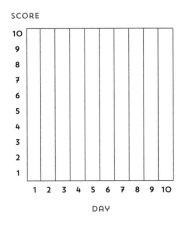

MY NEXT 10-DAY GOAL:

_____

_____

_____

_____

										BONUS

0%   10%   20%   30%   40%   50%   60%   70%   80%   90%   100%   125%

"TRUST THYSELF:
EVERY HEART VIBRATES TO
THAT IRON STRING."

—Ralph Waldo Emerson,
"Self-Reliance"

DAY 31

Date: _____

I am grateful for:

_____

_____

In 69 days, I will:

_____

_____

To achieve this, I will accomplish these three micro-goals today:

1. _____

2. _____

3. _____

My action plan for the day:

Task	Start Time	End Time
☐		
☐		
☐		
☐		
☐		

EVENING

Wonderful things that happened today:

_____

_____

_____

Three struggles I encountered:

1. _____

2. _____

3. _____

Possible solutions for these struggles:

1. _____

2. _____

3. _____

DISCIPLINE: 1 2 3 4 5   OVERALL DAY: 1 2 3 4 5

Am I closer to my goal today than I was yesterday?

☐ Yes   ☐ No

Final thought of the day:

_____

_____

_____

_____

_____

DAY 32

MORNING

I am grateful for:

_____

_____

In 68 days, I will:

_____

_____

To achieve this, I will accomplish these three micro-goals today:

1. _____

2. _____

3. _____

My action plan for the day:

Task	Start Time	End Time
☐		
☐		
☐		
☐		
☐		

Wonderful things that happened today:

_____

_____

_____

Three struggles I encountered:

1. _____

2. _____

3. _____

Possible solutions for these struggles:

1. _____

2. _____

3. _____

DISCIPLINE: 1 2 3 4 5   OVERALL DAY: 1 2 3 4 5

Am I closer to my goal today than I was yesterday?

☐ Yes   ☐ No

Final thought of the day:

_____

_____

_____

_____

_____

DAY 33

MORNING

I am grateful for:

_____

_____

In 67 days, I will:

_____

_____

To achieve this, I will accomplish these three micro-goals today:

1. _____

2. _____

3. _____

My action plan for the day:

Task	Start Time	End Time
☐		
☐		
☐		
☐		
☐		

EVENING

Wonderful things that happened today:

_____

_____

_____

Three struggles I encountered:

1. _____

2. _____

3. _____

Possible solutions for these struggles:

1. _____

2. _____

3. _____

DISCIPLINE: 1 2 3 4 5   OVERALL DAY: 1 2 3 4 5

Am I closer to my goal today than I was yesterday?

☐ Yes   ☐ No

Final thought of the day:

_____

_____

_____

_____

_____

DAY 34

Date: _____

I am grateful for:

_____

_____

In 66 days, I will:

_____

_____

To achieve this, I will accomplish these three micro-goals today:

1. _____

2. _____

3. _____

My action plan for the day:

Task	Start Time	End Time
☐		
☐		
☐		
☐		
☐		

Wonderful things that happened today:

_____

_____

_____

Three struggles I encountered:

1. _____

2. _____

3. _____

Possible solutions for these struggles:

1. _____

2. _____

3. _____

DISCIPLINE: 1 2 3 4 5   OVERALL DAY: 1 2 3 4 5

Am I closer to my goal today than I was yesterday?

☐ Yes   ☐ No

Final thought of the day:

_____

_____

_____

_____

_____

DAY 35

MORNING

I am grateful for:

_____

_____

In 65 days, I will:

_____

_____

To achieve this, I will accomplish these three micro-goals today:

1. _____

2. _____

3. _____

My action plan for the day:

Task	Start Time	End Time
☐		
☐		
☐		
☐		
☐		

Wonderful things that happened today:

_____

_____

_____

Three struggles I encountered:

1. _____

2. _____

3. _____

Possible solutions for these struggles:

1. _____

2. _____

3. _____

DISCIPLINE: 1 2 3 4 5   OVERALL DAY: 1 2 3 4 5

Am I closer to my goal today than I was yesterday?

☐ Yes   ☐ No

Final thought of the day:

_____

_____

_____

_____

_____

DAY 36

Date: _____

MORNING

I am grateful for:

_____

_____

In 64 days, I will:

_____

_____

To achieve this, I will accomplish these three micro-goals today:

1. _____

2. _____

3. _____

My action plan for the day:

Task	Start Time	End Time
☐		
☐		
☐		
☐		
☐		

EVENING

Wonderful things that happened today:

_____

_____

_____

Three struggles I encountered:

1. _____

2. _____

3. _____

Possible solutions for these struggles:

1. _____

2. _____

3. _____

DISCIPLINE: 1 2 3 4 5   OVERALL DAY: 1 2 3 4 5

Am I closer to my goal today than I was yesterday?

☐ Yes   ☐ No

Final thought of the day:

_____

_____

_____

_____

_____

DAY 37

Date: _____

I am grateful for:

_____

_____

In 63 days, I will:

_____

_____

To achieve this, I will accomplish these three micro-goals today:

1. _____

2. _____

3. _____

My action plan for the day:

Task	Start Time	End Time
☐		
☐		
☐		
☐		
☐		

Wonderful things that happened today:

_____

_____

_____

Three struggles I encountered:

1. _____

2. _____

3. _____

Possible solutions for these struggles:

1. _____

2. _____

3. _____

DISCIPLINE: 1 2 3 4 5   OVERALL DAY: 1 2 3 4 5

Am I closer to my goal today than I was yesterday?

☐ Yes   ☐ No

Final thought of the day:

_____

_____

_____

_____

_____

DAY 38

MORNING

I am grateful for:

_____

_____

In 62 days, I will:

_____

_____

To achieve this, I will accomplish these three micro-goals today:

1. _____

2. _____

3. _____

My action plan for the day:

Task	Start Time	End Time
☐		
☐		
☐		
☐		
☐		

Wonderful things that happened today:

_____

_____

_____

Three struggles I encountered:

1. _____

2. _____

3. _____

Possible solutions for these struggles:

1. _____

2. _____

3. _____

DISCIPLINE: 1 2 3 4 5 OVERALL DAY: 1 2 3 4 5

Am I closer to my goal today than I was yesterday?

☐ Yes   ☐ No

Final thought of the day:

_____

_____

_____

_____

_____

DAY 39

Date: _____

I am grateful for:

_____

_____

In 61 days, I will:

_____

_____

To achieve this, I will accomplish these three micro-goals today:

1. _____

2. _____

3. _____

My action plan for the day:

Task	Start Time	End Time
☐		
☐		
☐		
☐		
☐		

Wonderful things that happened today:

_____

_____

_____

Three struggles I encountered:

1. _____

2. _____

3. _____

Possible solutions for these struggles:

1. _____

2. _____

3. _____

DISCIPLINE: 1 2 3 4 5   OVERALL DAY: 1 2 3 4 5

Am I closer to my goal today than I was yesterday?

☐ Yes   ☐ No

Final thought of the day:

_____

_____

_____

_____

_____

DAY 40

Date: _____

I am grateful for:

_____

_____

In 60 days, I will:

_____

_____

To achieve this, I will accomplish these three micro-goals today:

1. _____

2. _____

3. _____

My action plan for the day:

Task	Start Time	End Time
☐		
☐		
☐		
☐		
☐		

EVENING

Wonderful things that happened today:

_____

_____

_____

Three struggles I encountered:

1. _____

2. _____

3. _____

Possible solutions for these struggles:

1. _____

2. _____

3. _____

DISCIPLINE: 1 2 3 4 5   OVERALL DAY: 1 2 3 4 5

Am I closer to my goal today than I was yesterday?

☐ Yes   ☐ No

Final thought of the day:

_____

_____

_____

_____

_____

10-DAY REVIEW

Did I accomplish my 10-day goal?

□ Yes   □ No

Three things that worked well over the last 10 days:

1. _____

2. _____

3. _____

My plan to amplify these wins:

1. _____

2. _____

3. _____

Three things that I struggled with over the last 10 days:

1. _____

2. _____

3. _____

My plan to fix these struggles:

1. _____

2. _____

3. _____

DISCIPLINE CHART

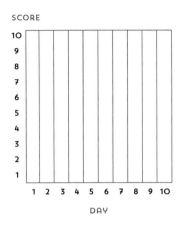

OVERALL DAY CHART

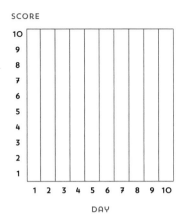

MY NEXT 10-DAY GOAL:

_____

_____

_____

_____

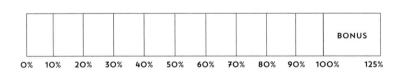

"AIM AT A HIGH MARK AND YOU'LL HIT IT.
NO, NOT THE FIRST TIME, NOR THE SECOND
TIME. MAYBE NOT THE THIRD. BUT KEEP ON
AIMING AND KEEP ON SHOOTING FOR ONLY
PRACTICE WILL MAKE YOU PERFECT."

—Annie Oakley

DAY 41

MORNING

I am grateful for:

_____

_____

In 59 days, I will:

_____

_____

To achieve this, I will accomplish these three micro-goals today:

1. _____

2. _____

3. _____

My action plan for the day:

Task	Start Time	End Time
☐		
☐		
☐		
☐		
☐		

EVENING

Wonderful things that happened today:

_____

_____

_____

Three struggles I encountered:

1. _____

2. _____

3. _____

Possible solutions for these struggles:

1. _____

2. _____

3. _____

DISCIPLINE: 1 2 3 4 5   OVERALL DAY: 1 2 3 4 5

Am I closer to my goal today than I was yesterday?

☐ Yes   ☐ No

Final thought of the day:

_____

_____

_____

_____

_____

DAY 42

Date: _____

MORNING

I am grateful for:

_____

_____

In 58 days, I will:

_____

_____

To achieve this, I will accomplish these three micro-goals today:

1. _____

2. _____

3. _____

My action plan for the day:

Task	Start Time	End Time
☐		
☐		
☐		
☐		
☐		

EVENING

Wonderful things that happened today:

_____

_____

_____

Three struggles I encountered:

1. _____

2. _____

3. _____

Possible solutions for these struggles:

1. _____

2. _____

3. _____

DISCIPLINE: 1 2 3 4 5 OVERALL DAY: 1 2 3 4 5

Am I closer to my goal today than I was yesterday?

☐ Yes   ☐ No

Final thought of the day:

_____

_____

_____

_____

_____

DAY 43

MORNING

I am grateful for:

_____

_____

In 57 days, I will:

_____

_____

To achieve this, I will accomplish these three micro-goals today:

1. _____

2. _____

3. _____

My action plan for the day:

Task	Start Time	End Time
☐		
☐		
☐		
☐		
☐		

EVENING

Wonderful things that happened today:

_____

_____

_____

Three struggles I encountered:

1. _____

2. _____

3. _____

Possible solutions for these struggles:

1. _____

2. _____

3. _____

DISCIPLINE: 1 2 3 4 5   OVERALL DAY: 1 2 3 4 5

Am I closer to my goal today than I was yesterday?

☐ Yes   ☐ No

Final thought of the day:

_____

_____

_____

_____

_____

DAY 44

Date: _____

MORNING

I am grateful for:

_____

_____

In 56 days, I will:

_____

_____

To achieve this, I will accomplish these three micro-goals today:

1. _____

2. _____

3. _____

My action plan for the day:

Task	Start Time	End Time
☐		
☐		
☐		
☐		
☐		

EVENING

Wonderful things that happened today:

_____

_____

_____

Three struggles I encountered:

1. _____

2. _____

3. _____

Possible solutions for these struggles:

1. _____

2. _____

3. _____

DISCIPLINE: 1 2 3 4 5   OVERALL DAY: 1 2 3 4 5

Am I closer to my goal today than I was yesterday?

☐ Yes   ☐ No

Final thought of the day:

_____

_____

_____

_____

_____

DAY 45

Date: _____

I am grateful for:

_____

_____

In 55 days, I will:

_____

_____

To achieve this, I will accomplish these three micro-goals today:

1. _____

2. _____

3. _____

My action plan for the day:

Task	Start Time	End Time
☐		
☐		
☐		
☐		
☐		

EVENING

Wonderful things that happened today:

_____

_____

_____

Three struggles I encountered:

1. _____

2. _____

3. _____

Possible solutions for these struggles:

1. _____

2. _____

3. _____

DISCIPLINE: 1 2 3 4 5   OVERALL DAY: 1 2 3 4 5

Am I closer to my goal today than I was yesterday?

☐ Yes   ☐ No

Final thought of the day:

_____

_____

_____

_____

_____

DAY 46

Date: _____

I am grateful for:

_____

_____

In 54 days, I will:

_____

_____

To achieve this, I will accomplish these three micro-goals today:

1. _____

2. _____

3. _____

My action plan for the day:

Task	Start Time	End Time
☐		
☐		
☐		
☐		
☐		

EVENING

Wonderful things that happened today:

_____

_____

_____

Three struggles I encountered:

1. _____

2. _____

3. _____

Possible solutions for these struggles:

1. _____

2. _____

3. _____

DISCIPLINE: 1 2 3 4 5   OVERALL DAY: 1 2 3 4 5

Am I closer to my goal today than I was yesterday?

☐ Yes   ☐ No

Final thought of the day:

_____

_____

_____

_____

_____

DAY 47

MORNING

I am grateful for:

_____

_____

In 53 days, I will:

_____

_____

To achieve this, I will accomplish these three micro-goals today:

1. _____

2. _____

3. _____

My action plan for the day:

Task	Start Time	End Time
☐		
☐		
☐		
☐		
☐		

EVENING

Wonderful things that happened today:

_____

_____

_____

Three struggles I encountered:

1. _____

2. _____

3. _____

Possible solutions for these struggles:

1. _____

2. _____

3. _____

DISCIPLINE: 1   2   3   4   5   OVERALL DAY: 1   2   3   4   5

Am I closer to my goal today than I was yesterday?

☐ Yes   ☐ No

Final thought of the day:

_____

_____

_____

_____

_____

DAY 48

Date: _____

MORNING

I am grateful for:

_____

_____

In 52 days, I will:

_____

_____

To achieve this, I will accomplish these three micro-goals today:

1. _____

2. _____

3. _____

My action plan for the day:

Task	Start Time	End Time
☐		
☐		
☐		
☐		
☐		

EVENING

Wonderful things that happened today:

_____

_____

_____

Three struggles I encountered:

1. _____

2. _____

3. _____

Possible solutions for these struggles:

1. _____

2. _____

3. _____

DISCIPLINE: 1 2 3 4 5   OVERALL DAY: 1 2 3 4 5

Am I closer to my goal today than I was yesterday?

☐ Yes   ☐ No

Final thought of the day:

_____

_____

_____

_____

_____

DAY 49

Date: _____

MORNING

I am grateful for:

_____

_____

In 51 days, I will:

_____

_____

To achieve this, I will accomplish these three micro-goals today:

1. _____

2. _____

3. _____

My action plan for the day:

Task	Start Time	End Time
☐		
☐		
☐		
☐		
☐		

EVENING

Wonderful things that happened today:

_____

_____

_____

Three struggles I encountered:

1. _____

2. _____

3. _____

Possible solutions for these struggles:

1. _____

2. _____

3. _____

DISCIPLINE: 1 2 3 4 5   OVERALL DAY: 1 2 3 4 5

Am I closer to my goal today than I was yesterday?

☐ Yes   ☐ No

Final thought of the day:

_____

_____

_____

_____

_____

DAY 50

Date: _____

MORNING

I am grateful for:

_____

_____

In 50 days, I will:

_____

_____

To achieve this, I will accomplish these three micro-goals today:

1. _____

2. _____

3. _____

My action plan for the day:

Task	Start Time	End Time
☐		
☐		
☐		
☐		
☐		

EVENING

Wonderful things that happened today:

_____

_____

_____

Three struggles I encountered:

1. _____

2. _____

3. _____

Possible solutions for these struggles:

1. _____

2. _____

3. _____

DISCIPLINE: 1 2 3 4 5   OVERALL DAY: 1 2 3 4 5

Am I closer to my goal today than I was yesterday?

□ Yes   □ No

Final thought of the day:

_____

_____

_____

_____

_____

10-DAY REVIEW

Did I accomplish my 10-day goal?

☐ Yes ☐ No

Three things that worked well over the last 10 days:

1. _____
2. _____
3. _____

My plan to amplify these wins:

1. _____
2. _____
3. _____

Three things that I struggled with over the last 10 days:

1. _____
2. _____
3. _____

My plan to fix these struggles:

1. _____
2. _____
3. _____

DISCIPLINE CHART

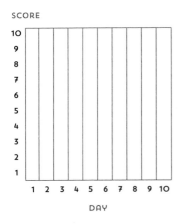

OVERALL DAY CHART

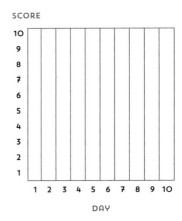

MY NEXT 10-DAY GOAL:

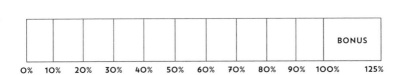

0%   10%   20%   30%   40%   50%   60%   70%   80%   90%   100%   125%

"THE SECRET OF MAN'S BEING IS
NOT ONLY TO LIVE BUT TO HAVE
SOMETHING TO LIVE FOR."

—Fyodor Dostoyevsky,
The Brothers Karamazov

DAY 51

MORNING

I am grateful for:

_____

_____

In 49 days, I will:

_____

_____

To achieve this, I will accomplish these three micro-goals today:

1. _____

2. _____

3. _____

My action plan for the day:

Task	Start Time	End Time
☐		
☐		
☐		
☐		
☐		

EVENING

Wonderful things that happened today:

_____

_____

_____

Three struggles I encountered:

1. _____

2. _____

3. _____

Possible solutions for these struggles:

1. _____

2. _____

3. _____

DISCIPLINE: 1 2 3 4 5   *OVERALL DAY:* 1 2 3 4 5

Am I closer to my goal today than I was yesterday?

☐ Yes   ☐ No

Final thought of the day:

_____

_____

_____

_____

_____

DAY 52

Date: _____

MORNING

I am grateful for:

_____

_____

In 48 days, I will:

_____

_____

To achieve this, I will accomplish these three micro-goals today:

1. _____

2. _____

3. _____

My action plan for the day:

Task	Start Time	End Time
☐		
☐		
☐		
☐		
☐		

EVENING

Wonderful things that happened today:

_____

_____

_____

Three struggles I encountered:

1. _____

2. _____

3. _____

Possible solutions for these struggles:

1. _____

2. _____

3. _____

DISCIPLINE: 1 2 3 4 5   OVERALL DAY: 1 2 3 4 5

Am I closer to my goal today than I was yesterday?

☐ Yes   ☐ No

Final thought of the day:

_____

_____

_____

_____

_____

DAY 53

MORNING

I am grateful for:

_____

_____

In 47 days, I will:

_____

_____

To achieve this, I will accomplish these three micro-goals today:

1. _____

2. _____

3. _____

My action plan for the day:

Task	Start Time	End Time
☐		
☐		
☐		
☐		
☐		

EVENING

Wonderful things that happened today:

_____

_____

_____

Three struggles I encountered:

1. _____

2. _____

3. _____

Possible solutions for these struggles:

1. _____

2. _____

3. _____

DISCIPLINE: 1 2 3 4 5   OVERALL DAY: 1 2 3 4 5

Am I closer to my goal today than I was yesterday?

☐ Yes   ☐ No

Final thought of the day:

_____

_____

_____

_____

_____

DAY 54

MORNING

I am grateful for:

_____

_____

In 46 days, I will:

_____

_____

To achieve this, I will accomplish these three micro-goals today:

1. _____

2. _____

3. _____

My action plan for the day:

Task	Start Time	End Time
☐		
☐		
☐		
☐		
☐		

EVENING

Wonderful things that happened today:

_____

_____

_____

Three struggles I encountered:

1. _____

2. _____

3. _____

Possible solutions for these struggles:

1. _____

2. _____

3. _____

DISCIPLINE: 1 2 3 4 5   OVERALL DAY: 1 2 3 4 5

Am I closer to my goal today than I was yesterday?

☐ Yes   ☐ No

Final thought of the day:

_____

_____

_____

_____

_____

DAY 55

Date: _____

MORNING

I am grateful for:

_____

_____

In 45 days, I will:

_____

_____

To achieve this, I will accomplish these three micro-goals today:

1. _____

2. _____

3. _____

My action plan for the day:

Task	Start Time	End Time
☐		
☐		
☐		
☐		
☐		

EVENING

Wonderful things that happened today:

_____

_____

_____

Three struggles I encountered:

1. _____

2. _____

3. _____

Possible solutions for these struggles:

1. _____

2. _____

3. _____

DISCIPLINE: 1 2 3 4 5   OVERALL DAY: 1 2 3 4 5

Am I closer to my goal today than I was yesterday?

☐ Yes   ☐ No

Final thought of the day:

_____

_____

_____

_____

_____

DAY 56

Date: _____

MORNING

I am grateful for:

_____

_____

In 44 days, I will:

_____

_____

To achieve this, I will accomplish these three micro-goals today:

1. _____

2. _____

3. _____

My action plan for the day:

Task	Start Time	End Time
☐		
☐		
☐		
☐		
☐		

EVENING

Wonderful things that happened today:

_____

_____

_____

Three struggles I encountered:

1. _____

2. _____

3. _____

Possible solutions for these struggles:

1. _____

2. _____

3. _____

DISCIPLINE: 1 2 3 4 5   *OVERALL DAY:* 1 2 3 4 5

Am I closer to my goal today than I was yesterday?

☐ Yes   ☐ No

Final thought of the day:

_____

_____

_____

_____

_____

DAY 57

Date: _____

I am grateful for:

_____

_____

In 43 days, I will:

_____

_____

To achieve this, I will accomplish these three micro-goals today:

1. _____

2. _____

3. _____

My action plan for the day:

Task	Start Time	End Time
☐		
☐		
☐		
☐		
☐		

EVENING

Wonderful things that happened today:

_____

_____

_____

Three struggles I encountered:

1. _____

2. _____

3. _____

Possible solutions for these struggles:

1. _____

2. _____

3. _____

DISCIPLINE: 1 2 3 4 5   OVERALL DAY: 1 2 3 4 5

Am I closer to my goal today than I was yesterday?

☐ Yes   ☐ No

Final thought of the day:

_____

_____

_____

_____

_____

DAY 58

Date: _____

MORNING

I am grateful for:

_____

_____

In 42 days, I will:

_____

_____

To achieve this, I will accomplish these three micro-goals today:

1. _____

2. _____

3. _____

My action plan for the day:

Task	Start Time	End Time
☐		
☐		
☐		
☐		
☐		

EVENING

Wonderful things that happened today:

_____

_____

_____

Three struggles I encountered:

1. _____

2. _____

3. _____

Possible solutions for these struggles:

1. _____

2. _____

3. _____

DISCIPLINE: 1 2 3 4 5   OVERALL DAY: 1 2 3 4 5

Am I closer to my goal today than I was yesterday?

☐ Yes   ☐ No

Final thought of the day:

_____

_____

_____

_____

_____

DAY 59

Date: _____

MORNING

I am grateful for:

_____

_____

In 41 days, I will:

_____

_____

To achieve this, I will accomplish these three micro-goals today:

1. _____

2. _____

3. _____

My action plan for the day:

Task	Start Time	End Time
☐		
☐		
☐		
☐		
☐		

EVENING

Wonderful things that happened today:

_____

_____

_____

Three struggles I encountered:

1. _____

2. _____

3. _____

Possible solutions for these struggles:

1. _____

2. _____

3. _____

DISCIPLINE: 1 2 3 4 5   OVERALL DAY: 1 2 3 4 5

Am I closer to my goal today than I was yesterday?

☐ Yes   ☐ No

Final thought of the day:

_____

_____

_____

_____

_____

# DAY 60

Date: _____

MORNING

I am grateful for:

_____

_____

In 40 days, I will:

_____

_____

To achieve this, I will accomplish these three micro-goals today:

1. _____

2. _____

3. _____

My action plan for the day:

Task	Start Time	End Time
☐		
☐		
☐		
☐		
☐		

EVENING

Wonderful things that happened today:

_____

_____

_____

Three struggles I encountered:

1. _____

2. _____

3. _____

Possible solutions for these struggles:

1. _____

2. _____

3. _____

DISCIPLINE: 1 2 3 4 5   OVERALL DAY: 1 2 3 4 5

Am I closer to my goal today than I was yesterday?

☐ Yes   ☐ No

Final thought of the day:

_____

_____

_____

_____

_____

10-DAY REVIEW

Did I accomplish my 10-day goal?

□ Yes   □ No

Three things that worked well over the last 10 days:

1. _____

2. _____

3. _____

My plan to amplify these wins:

1. _____

2. _____

3. _____

Three things that I struggled with over the last 10 days:

1. _____

2. _____

3. _____

My plan to fix these struggles:

1. _____

2. _____

3. _____

DISCIPLINE CHART

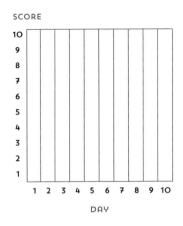

SCORE

10
9
8
7
6
5
4
3
2
1

1 2 3 4 5 6 7 8 9 10

DAY

OVERALL DAY CHART

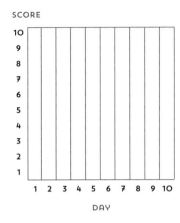

SCORE

10
9
8
7
6
5
4
3
2
1

1 2 3 4 5 6 7 8 9 10

DAY

MY NEXT 10-DAY GOAL:

_____

_____

_____

_____

										BONUS

0% 10% 20% 30% 40% 50% 60% 70% 80% 90% 100% 125%

"STRONG REASONS MAKE
STRONG ACTIONS."

—William Shakespeare,
The Life and Death of King John

DAY 61

MORNING

I am grateful for:

_____

_____

In 39 days, I will:

_____

_____

To achieve this, I will accomplish these three micro-goals today:

1. _____

2. _____

3. _____

My action plan for the day:

Task	Start Time	End Time
☐		
☐		
☐		
☐		
☐		

EVENING

Wonderful things that happened today:

_____

_____

_____

Three struggles I encountered:

1. _____

2. _____

3. _____

Possible solutions for these struggles:

1. _____

2. _____

3. _____

DISCIPLINE: 1 2 3 4 5   OVERALL DAY: 1 2 3 4 5

Am I closer to my goal today than I was yesterday?

☐ Yes   ☐ No

Final thought of the day:

_____

_____

_____

_____

_____

DAY 62

Date: _____

I am grateful for:

_____

_____

In 38 days, I will:

_____

_____

To achieve this, I will accomplish these three micro-goals today:

1. _____

2. _____

3. _____

My action plan for the day:

Task	Start Time	End Time
☐		
☐		
☐		
☐		
☐		

EVENING

Wonderful things that happened today:

_____

_____

_____

Three struggles I encountered:

1. _____

2. _____

3. _____

Possible solutions for these struggles:

1. _____

2. _____

3. _____

DISCIPLINE: 1 2 3 4 5   *OVERALL DAY:* 1 2 3 4 5

Am I closer to my goal today than I was yesterday?

☐ Yes   ☐ No

Final thought of the day:

_____

_____

_____

_____

_____

DAY 63

Date: _____

I am grateful for:

_____

_____

In 37 days, I will:

_____

_____

To achieve this, I will accomplish these three micro-goals today:

1. _____

2. _____

3. _____

My action plan for the day:

Task	Start Time	End Time
☐		
☐		
☐		
☐		
☐		

EVENING

Wonderful things that happened today:

_____

_____

_____

Three struggles I encountered:

1. _____

2. _____

3. _____

Possible solutions for these struggles:

1. _____

2. _____

3. _____

DISCIPLINE: 1 2 3 4 5   OVERALL DAY: 1 2 3 4 5

Am I closer to my goal today than I was yesterday?

☐ Yes   ☐ No

Final thought of the day:

_____

_____

_____

_____

_____

DAY 64

Date: _____

MORNING

I am grateful for:

_____

_____

In 36 days, I will:

_____

_____

To achieve this, I will accomplish these three micro-goals today:

1. _____

2. _____

3. _____

My action plan for the day:

Task	Start Time	End Time
☐		
☐		
☐		
☐		
☐		

EVENING

Wonderful things that happened today:

_____

_____

_____

Three struggles I encountered:

1. _____

2. _____

3. _____

Possible solutions for these struggles:

1. _____

2. _____

3. _____

DISCIPLINE: 1 2 3 4 5   OVERALL DAY: 1 2 3 4 5

Am I closer to my goal today than I was yesterday?

☐ Yes   ☐ No

Final thought of the day:

_____

_____

_____

_____

_____

DAY 65

Date: _____

I am grateful for:

_____

_____

In 35 days, I will:

_____

_____

To achieve this, I will accomplish these three micro-goals today:

1. _____

2. _____

3. _____

My action plan for the day:

Task	Start Time	End Time
☐		
☐		
☐		
☐		
☐		

EVENING

Wonderful things that happened today:

_____

_____

_____

Three struggles I encountered:

1. _____

2. _____

3. _____

Possible solutions for these struggles:

1. _____

2. _____

3. _____

DISCIPLINE: 1 2 3 4 5   OVERALL DAY: 1 2 3 4 5

Am I closer to my goal today than I was yesterday?

☐ Yes   ☐ No

Final thought of the day:

_____

_____

_____

_____

_____

DAY 66

Date: _____

I am grateful for:

_____

_____

In 34 days, I will:

_____

_____

To achieve this, I will accomplish these three micro-goals today:

1. _____

2. _____

3. _____

My action plan for the day:

Task	Start Time	End Time
☐		
☐		
☐		
☐		
☐		

EVENING

Wonderful things that happened today:

_____

_____

_____

Three struggles I encountered:

1. _____

2. _____

3. _____

Possible solutions for these struggles:

1. _____

2. _____

3. _____

DISCIPLINE: 1 2 3 4 5   OVERALL DAY: 1 2 3 4 5

Am I closer to my goal today than I was yesterday?

☐ Yes   ☐ No

Final thought of the day:

_____

_____

_____

_____

_____

DAY 67

Date: _____

MORNING

I am grateful for:

_____

_____

In 33 days, I will:

_____

_____

To achieve this, I will accomplish these three micro-goals today:

1. _____

2. _____

3. _____

My action plan for the day:

Task	Start Time	End Time
☐		
☐		
☐		
☐		
☐		

EVENING

Wonderful things that happened today:

_____

_____

_____

Three struggles I encountered:

1. _____

2. _____

3. _____

Possible solutions for these struggles:

1. _____

2. _____

3. _____

DISCIPLINE: 1 2 3 4 5 *OVERALL DAY:* 1 2 3 4 5

Am I closer to my goal today than I was yesterday?

☐ Yes   ☐ No

Final thought of the day:

_____

_____

_____

_____

_____

DAY 68

MORNING

I am grateful for:

_____

_____

In 32 days, I will:

_____

_____

To achieve this, I will accomplish these three micro-goals today:

1. _____

2. _____

3. _____

My action plan for the day:

Task	Start Time	End Time
☐		
☐		
☐		
☐		
☐		

EVENING

Wonderful things that happened today:

_____

_____

_____

Three struggles I encountered:

1. _____

2. _____

3. _____

Possible solutions for these struggles:

1. _____

2. _____

3. _____

DISCIPLINE: 1 2 3 4 5   OVERALL DAY: 1 2 3 4 5

Am I closer to my goal today than I was yesterday?

☐ Yes   ☐ No

Final thought of the day:

_____

_____

_____

_____

_____

DAY 69

Date: _____

MORNING

I am grateful for:

_____

_____

In 31 days, I will:

_____

_____

To achieve this, I will accomplish these three micro-goals today:

1. _____

2. _____

3. _____

My action plan for the day:

Task	Start Time	End Time
☐		
☐		
☐		
☐		
☐		

EVENING

Wonderful things that happened today:

_____

_____

_____

Three struggles I encountered:

1. _____

2. _____

3. _____

Possible solutions for these struggles:

1. _____

2. _____

3. _____

DISCIPLINE: 1 2 3 4 5   OVERALL DAY: 1 2 3 4 5

Am I closer to my goal today than I was yesterday?

☐ Yes   ☐ No

Final thought of the day:

_____

_____

_____

_____

_____

DAY 70

Date: _____

MORNING

I am grateful for:

_____

_____

In 30 days, I will:

_____

_____

To achieve this, I will accomplish these three micro-goals today:

1. _____

2. _____

3. _____

My action plan for the day:

Task	Start Time	End Time
☐		
☐		
☐		
☐		
☐		

EVENING

Wonderful things that happened today:

_____

_____

_____

Three struggles I encountered:

1. _____

2. _____

3. _____

Possible solutions for these struggles:

1. _____

2. _____

3. _____

DISCIPLINE: 1 2 3 4 5   OVERALL DAY: 1 2 3 4 5

Am I closer to my goal today than I was yesterday?

☐ Yes   ☐ No

Final thought of the day:

_____

_____

_____

_____

_____

10-DAY REVIEW

Did I accomplish my 10-day goal?

☐ Yes ☐ No

Three things that worked well over the last 10 days:

1. _____

2. _____

3. _____

My plan to amplify these wins:

1. _____

2. _____

3. _____

Three things that I struggled with over the last 10 days:

1. _____

2. _____

3. _____

My plan to fix these struggles:

1. _____

2. _____

3. _____

DISCIPLINE CHART

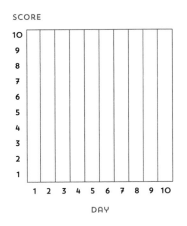

OVERALL DAY CHART

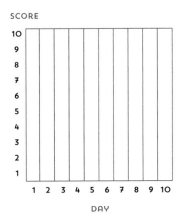

MY NEXT 10-DAY GOAL:

_____

_____

_____

_____

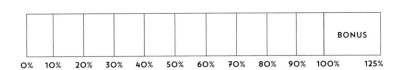

"KNOW YOUR OWN HAPPINESS. YOU WANT NOTHING BUT PATIENCE—OR GIVE IT A MORE FASCINATING NAME, CALL IT HOPE."

—Jane Austen, *Sense and Sensibility*

DAY 71

Date: _____

MORNING

I am grateful for:

_____

_____

In 29 days, I will:

_____

_____

To achieve this, I will accomplish these three micro-goals today:

1. _____

2. _____

3. _____

My action plan for the day:

Task	Start Time	End Time
☐		
☐		
☐		
☐		
☐		

EVENING

Wonderful things that happened today:

_____

_____

_____

Three struggles I encountered:

1. _____

2. _____

3. _____

Possible solutions for these struggles:

1. _____

2. _____

3. _____

DISCIPLINE: 1 2 3 4 5   OVERALL DAY: 1 2 3 4 5

Am I closer to my goal today than I was yesterday?

☐ Yes   ☐ No

Final thought of the day:

_____

_____

_____

_____

_____

DAY 72

Date: _____

I am grateful for:

_____

_____

In 28 days, I will:

_____

_____

To achieve this, I will accomplish these three micro-goals today:

1. _____

2. _____

3. _____

My action plan for the day:

Task	Start Time	End Time
☐		
☐		
☐		
☐		
☐		

Wonderful things that happened today:

_____

_____

_____

Three struggles I encountered:

1. _____

2. _____

3. _____

Possible solutions for these struggles:

1. _____

2. _____

3. _____

DISCIPLINE: 1 2 3 4 5   OVERALL DAY: 1 2 3 4 5

Am I closer to my goal today than I was yesterday?

☐ Yes   ☐ No

Final thought of the day:

_____

_____

_____

_____

_____

DAY 73

MORNING

I am grateful for:

_____

_____

In 27 days, I will:

_____

_____

To achieve this, I will accomplish these three micro-goals today:

1. _____

2. _____

3. _____

My action plan for the day:

Task	Start Time	End Time
☐		
☐		
☐		
☐		
☐		

EVENING

Wonderful things that happened today:

_____

_____

_____

Three struggles I encountered:

1. _____

2. _____

3. _____

Possible solutions for these struggles:

1. _____

2. _____

3. _____

DISCIPLINE: 1 2 3 4 5   OVERALL DAY: 1 2 3 4 5

Am I closer to my goal today than I was yesterday?

☐ Yes   ☐ No

Final thought of the day:

_____

_____

_____

_____

_____

DAY 74

MORNING

I am grateful for:

_____

_____

In 26 days, I will:

_____

_____

To achieve this, I will accomplish these three micro-goals today:

1. _____

2. _____

3. _____

My action plan for the day:

Task	Start Time	End Time
☐		
☐		
☐		
☐		
☐		

EVENING

Wonderful things that happened today:

_____

_____

_____

Three struggles I encountered:

1. _____

2. _____

3. _____

Possible solutions for these struggles:

1. _____

2. _____

3. _____

DISCIPLINE: 1 2 3 4 5   OVERALL DAY: 1 2 3 4 5

Am I closer to my goal today than I was yesterday?

☐ Yes   ☐ No

Final thought of the day:

_____

_____

_____

_____

_____

DAY 75

Date: _____

MORNING

I am grateful for:

_____

_____

In 25 days, I will:

_____

_____

To achieve this, I will accomplish these three micro-goals today:

1. _____

2. _____

3. _____

My action plan for the day:

Task	Start Time	End Time
☐		
☐		
☐		
☐		
☐		

EVENING

Wonderful things that happened today:

_____

_____

_____

Three struggles I encountered:

1. _____

2. _____

3. _____

Possible solutions for these struggles:

1. _____

2. _____

3. _____

DISCIPLINE: 1 2 3 4 5   OVERALL DAY: 1 2 3 4 5

Am I closer to my goal today than I was yesterday?

☐ Yes   ☐ No

Final thought of the day:

_____

_____

_____

_____

_____

DAY 76

Date: _____

I am grateful for:

_____

_____

In 24 days, I will:

_____

_____

To achieve this, I will accomplish these three micro-goals today:

1. _____

2. _____

3. _____

My action plan for the day:

Task	Start Time	End Time
☐		
☐		
☐		
☐		
☐		

EVENING

Wonderful things that happened today:

_____

_____

_____

Three struggles I encountered:

1. _____

2. _____

3. _____

Possible solutions for these struggles:

1. _____

2. _____

3. _____

DISCIPLINE: 1 2 3 4 5   OVERALL DAY: 1 2 3 4 5

Am I closer to my goal today than I was yesterday?

☐ Yes   ☐ No

Final thought of the day:

_____

_____

_____

_____

_____

DAY 77

MORNING

I am grateful for:

_____

_____

In 23 days, I will:

_____

_____

To achieve this, I will accomplish these three micro-goals today:

1. _____

2. _____

3. _____

My action plan for the day:

Task	Start Time	End Time
☐		
☐		
☐		
☐		
☐		

EVENING

Wonderful things that happened today:

_____

_____

_____

Three struggles I encountered:

1. _____

2. _____

3. _____

Possible solutions for these struggles:

1. _____

2. _____

3. _____

DISCIPLINE: 1 2 3 4 5   OVERALL DAY: 1 2 3 4 5

Am I closer to my goal today than I was yesterday?

☐ Yes   ☐ No

Final thought of the day:

_____

_____

_____

_____

_____

DAY 78

MORNING

I am grateful for:

_____

_____

In 22 days, I will:

_____

_____

To achieve this, I will accomplish these three micro-goals today:

1. _____

2. _____

3. _____

My action plan for the day:

Task	Start Time	End Time
☐		
☐		
☐		
☐		
☐		

EVENING

Wonderful things that happened today:

_____

_____

_____

Three struggles I encountered:

1. _____

2. _____

3. _____

Possible solutions for these struggles:

1. _____

2. _____

3. _____

DISCIPLINE: 1 2 3 4 5   OVERALL DAY: 1 2 3 4 5

Am I closer to my goal today than I was yesterday?

☐ Yes   ☐ No

Final thought of the day:

_____

_____

_____

_____

_____

DAY 79

MORNING

I am grateful for:

_____

_____

In 21 days, I will:

_____

_____

To achieve this, I will accomplish these three micro-goals today:

1. _____

2. _____

3. _____

My action plan for the day:

Task	Start Time	End Time
☐		
☐		
☐		
☐		
☐		

EVENING

Wonderful things that happened today:

_____

_____

_____

Three struggles I encountered:

1. _____

2. _____

3. _____

Possible solutions for these struggles:

1. _____

2. _____

3. _____

DISCIPLINE: 1 2 3 4 5   OVERALL DAY: 1 2 3 4 5

Am I closer to my goal today than I was yesterday?

☐ Yes   ☐ No

Final thought of the day:

_____

_____

_____

_____

_____

DAY 80

Date: _____

MORNING

I am grateful for:

_____

_____

In 20 days, I will:

_____

_____

To achieve this, I will accomplish these three micro-goals today:

1. _____

2. _____

3. _____

My action plan for the day:

Task	Start Time	End Time
☐		
☐		
☐		
☐		
☐		

EVENING

Wonderful things that happened today:

_____

_____

_____

Three struggles I encountered:

1. _____

2. _____

3. _____

Possible solutions for these struggles:

1. _____

2. _____

3. _____

DISCIPLINE: 1 2 3 4 5   *OVERALL DAY:* 1 2 3 4 5

Am I closer to my goal today than I was yesterday?

☐ Yes   ☐ No

Final thought of the day:

_____

_____

_____

_____

_____

10-DAY REVIEW

Did I accomplish my 10-day goal?

☐ Yes   ☐ No

Three things that worked well over the last 10 days:

1. _____

2. _____

3. _____

My plan to amplify these wins:

1. _____

2. _____

3. _____

Three things that I struggled with over the last 10 days:

1. _____

2. _____

3. _____

My plan to fix these struggles:

1. _____

2. _____

3. _____

DISCIPLINE CHART

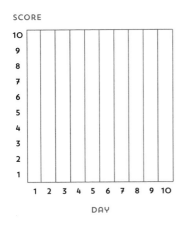

SCORE

10
9
8
7
6
5
4
3
2
1

1 2 3 4 5 6 7 8 9 10

DAY

OVERALL DAY CHART

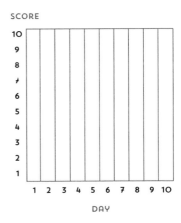

SCORE

10
9
8
7
6
5
4
3
2
1

1 2 3 4 5 6 7 8 9 10

DAY

MY NEXT 10-DAY GOAL:

_____

_____

_____

_____

										BONUS

0% 10% 20% 30% 40% 50% 60% 70% 80% 90% 100% 125%

"NOTHING CONTRIBUTES SO MUCH
TO TRANQUILIZE THE MIND AS
A STEADY PURPOSE."

—Mary Shelley, *Frankenstein*

DAY 81

Date: _____

I am grateful for:

_____

_____

In 19 days, I will:

_____

_____

To achieve this, I will accomplish these three micro-goals today:

1. _____

2. _____

3. _____

My action plan for the day:

Task	Start Time	End Time
☐		
☐		
☐		
☐		
☐		

EVENING

Wonderful things that happened today:

_____

_____

_____

Three struggles I encountered:

1. _____

2. _____

3. _____

Possible solutions for these struggles:

1. _____

2. _____

3. _____

DISCIPLINE: 1 2 3 4 5   OVERALL DAY: 1 2 3 4 5

Am I closer to my goal today than I was yesterday?

☐ Yes   ☐ No

Final thought of the day:

_____

_____

_____

_____

_____

DAY 82

Date: _____

I am grateful for:

_____

_____

In 18 days, I will:

_____

_____

To achieve this, I will accomplish these three micro-goals today:

1. _____

2. _____

3. _____

My action plan for the day:

Task	Start Time	End Time
☐		
☐		
☐		
☐		
☐		

EVENING

Wonderful things that happened today:

_____

_____

_____

Three struggles I encountered:

1. _____

2. _____

3. _____

Possible solutions for these struggles:

1. _____

2. _____

3. _____

DISCIPLINE: 1 2 3 4 5   OVERALL DAY: 1 2 3 4 5

Am I closer to my goal today than I was yesterday?

☐ Yes   ☐ No

Final thought of the day:

_____

_____

_____

_____

_____

DAY 83

Date: _____

I am grateful for:

_____

_____

In 17 days, I will:

_____

_____

To achieve this, I will accomplish these three micro-goals today:

1. _____

2. _____

3. _____

My action plan for the day:

Task	Start Time	End Time
☐		
☐		
☐		
☐		
☐		

Wonderful things that happened today:

_____

_____

_____

Three struggles I encountered:

1. _____

2. _____

3. _____

Possible solutions for these struggles:

1. _____

2. _____

3. _____

DISCIPLINE: 1 2 3 4 5 OVERALL DAY: 1 2 3 4 5

Am I closer to my goal today than I was yesterday?

☐ Yes   ☐ No

Final thought of the day:

_____

_____

_____

_____

_____

DAY 84

Date: _____

MORNING

I am grateful for:

_____

_____

In 16 days, I will:

_____

_____

To achieve this, I will accomplish these three micro-goals today:

1. _____

2. _____

3. _____

My action plan for the day:

Task	Start Time	End Time
☐		
☐		
☐		
☐		
☐		

EVENING

Wonderful things that happened today:

_____

_____

_____   _____

Three struggles I encountered:

1. _____

2. _____

3. _____

Possible solutions for these struggles:

1. _____

2. _____

3. _____

DISCIPLINE: 1 2 3 4 5   OVERALL DAY: 1 2 3 4 5

Am I closer to my goal today than I was yesterday?

☐ Yes   ☐ No

Final thought of the day:

_____

_____

_____

_____

_____

DAY 85

Date: _____

I am grateful for:

_____

_____

In 15 days, I will:

_____

_____

To achieve this, I will accomplish these three micro-goals today:

1. _____

2. _____

3. _____

My action plan for the day:

Task	Start Time	End Time
☐		
☐		
☐		
☐		
☐		

EVENING

Wonderful things that happened today:

_____

_____

_____

Three struggles I encountered:

1. _____

2. _____

3. _____

Possible solutions for these struggles:

1. _____

2. _____

3. _____

DISCIPLINE: 1 2 3 4 5   OVERALL DAY: 1 2 3 4 5

Am I closer to my goal today than I was yesterday?

☐ Yes   ☐ No

Final thought of the day:

_____

_____

_____

_____

_____

DAY 86

Date: _____

MORNING

I am grateful for:

_____

_____

In 14 days, I will:

_____

_____

To achieve this, I will accomplish these three micro-goals today:

1. _____

2. _____

3. _____

My action plan for the day:

Task	Start Time	End Time
☐		
☐		
☐		
☐		
☐		

EVENING

Wonderful things that happened today:

_____

_____

_____

Three struggles I encountered:

1. _____

2. _____

3. _____

Possible solutions for these struggles:

1. _____

2. _____

3. _____

DISCIPLINE: 1 2 3 4 5   OVERALL DAY: 1 2 3 4 5

Am I closer to my goal today than I was yesterday?

☐ Yes   ☐ No

Final thought of the day:

_____

_____

_____

_____

_____

DAY 87

Date: _____

MORNING

I am grateful for:

_____

_____

In 13 days, I will:

_____

_____

To achieve this, I will accomplish these three micro-goals today:

1. _____

2. _____

3. _____

My action plan for the day:

Task	Start Time	End Time
☐		
☐		
☐		
☐		
☐		

Wonderful things that happened today:

_____

_____

_____

Three struggles I encountered:

1. _____

2. _____

3. _____

Possible solutions for these struggles:

1. _____

2. _____

3. _____

DISCIPLINE: 1 2 3 4 5   OVERALL DAY: 1 2 3 4 5

Am I closer to my goal today than I was yesterday?

☐ Yes   ☐ No

Final thought of the day:

_____

_____

_____

_____

_____

DAY 88

Date: _____

MORNING

I am grateful for:

_____

_____

In 12 days, I will:

_____

_____

To achieve this, I will accomplish these three micro-goals today:

1. _____

2. _____

3. _____

My action plan for the day:

Task	Start Time	End Time
☐		
☐		
☐		
☐		
☐		

EVENING

Wonderful things that happened today:

_____

_____

_____

Three struggles I encountered:

1. _____

2. _____

3. _____

Possible solutions for these struggles:

1. _____

2. _____

3. _____

DISCIPLINE: 1 2 3 4 5   OVERALL DAY: 1 2 3 4 5

Am I closer to my goal today than I was yesterday?

☐ Yes   ☐ No

Final thought of the day:

_____

_____

_____

_____

_____

DAY 89

MORNING

I am grateful for:

_____

_____

In 11 days, I will:

_____

_____

To achieve this, I will accomplish these three micro-goals today:

1. _____

2. _____

3. _____

My action plan for the day:

Task	Start Time	End Time
☐		
☐		
☐		
☐		
☐		

EVENING

Wonderful things that happened today:

_____

_____

_____

Three struggles I encountered:

1. _____

2. _____

3. _____

Possible solutions for these struggles:

1. _____

2. _____

3. _____

DISCIPLINE: 1 2 3 4 5   OVERALL DAY: 1 2 3 4 5

Am I closer to my goal today than I was yesterday?

☐ Yes   ☐ No

Final thought of the day:

_____

_____

_____

_____

_____

DAY 90

Date: _____

MORNING

I am grateful for:

_____

_____

In 10 days, I will:

_____

_____

To achieve this, I will accomplish these three micro-goals today:

1. _____

2. _____

3. _____

My action plan for the day:

Task	Start Time	End Time
☐		
☐		
☐		
☐		
☐		

EVENING

Wonderful things that happened today:

_____

_____

_____

Three struggles I encountered:

1. _____

2. _____

3. _____

Possible solutions for these struggles:

1. _____

2. _____

3. _____

DISCIPLINE: 1 2 3 4 5   OVERALL DAY: 1 2 3 4 5

Am I closer to my goal today than I was yesterday?

☐ Yes   ☐ No

Final thought of the day:

_____

_____

_____

_____

_____

10-DAY REVIEW

Did I accomplish my 10-day goal?

□ Yes   □ No

Three things that worked well over the last 10 days:

1. _____

2. _____

3. _____

My plan to amplify these wins:

1. _____

2. _____

3. _____

Three things that I struggled with over the last 10 days:

1. _____

2. _____

3. _____

My plan to fix these struggles:

1. _____

2. _____

3. _____

DISCIPLINE CHART

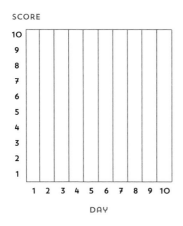

SCORE

DAY

OVERALL DAY CHART

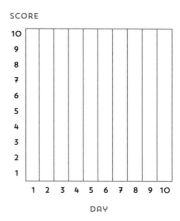

SCORE

DAY

MY NEXT 10-DAY GOAL:

_____

_____

_____

_____

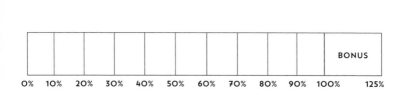

BONUS

0% 10% 20% 30% 40% 50% 60% 70% 80% 90% 100% 125%

"WHEN YOU GET INTO A TIGHT PLACE,
AND EVERYTHING GOES AGAINST YOU TILL
IT SEEMS AS IF YOU COULDN'T HOLD ON
A MINUTE LONGER, NEVER GIVE UP THEN,
FOR THAT'S JUST THE PLACE AND TIME
THAT THE TIDE'LL TURN."

—Harriet Beecher Stowe

DAY 91

Date: _____

I am grateful for:

_____

_____

In 9 days, I will:

_____

_____

To achieve this, I will accomplish these three micro-goals today:

1. _____

2. _____

3. _____

My action plan for the day:

Task	Start Time	End Time
☐		
☐		
☐		
☐		
☐		

EVENING

Wonderful things that happened today:

_____

_____

_____

Three struggles I encountered:

1. _____

2. _____

3. _____

Possible solutions for these struggles:

1. _____

2. _____

3. _____

DISCIPLINE: 1 2 3 4 5   OVERALL DAY: 1 2 3 4 5

Am I closer to my goal today than I was yesterday?

☐ Yes   ☐ No

Final thought of the day:

_____

_____

_____

_____

_____

DAY 92

MORNING

I am grateful for:

_____

_____

In 8 days, I will:

_____

_____

To achieve this, I will accomplish these three micro-goals today:

1. _____

2. _____

3. _____

My action plan for the day:

Task	Start Time	End Time
☐		
☐		
☐		
☐		
☐		

EVENING

Wonderful things that happened today:

_____

_____

_____

Three struggles I encountered:

1. _____

2. _____

3. _____

Possible solutions for these struggles:

1. _____

2. _____

3. _____

DISCIPLINE: 1 2 3 4 5   OVERALL DAY: 1 2 3 4 5

Am I closer to my goal today than I was yesterday?

☐ Yes   ☐ No

Final thought of the day:

_____

_____

_____

_____

_____

DAY 93

Date: _____

MORNING

I am grateful for:

_____

_____

In 7 days, I will:

_____

_____

To achieve this, I will accomplish these three micro-goals today:

1. _____

2. _____

3. _____

My action plan for the day:

Task	Start Time	End Time
☐		
☐		
☐		
☐		
☐		

EVENING

Wonderful things that happened today:

_____

_____

_____

Three struggles I encountered:

1. _____

2. _____

3. _____

Possible solutions for these struggles:

1. _____

2. _____

3. _____

DISCIPLINE: 1 2 3 4 5   OVERALL DAY: 1 2 3 4 5

Am I closer to my goal today than I was yesterday?

☐ Yes   ☐ No

Final thought of the day:

_____

_____

_____

_____

_____

DAY 94

Date: _____

MORNING

I am grateful for:

_____

_____

In 6 days, I will:

_____

_____

To achieve this, I will accomplish these three micro-goals today:

1. _____

2. _____

3. _____

My action plan for the day:

Task	Start Time	End Time
☐		
☐		
☐		
☐		
☐		

EVENING

Wonderful things that happened today:

_____

_____

_____

Three struggles I encountered:

1. _____

2. _____

3. _____

Possible solutions for these struggles:

1. _____

2. _____

3. _____

DISCIPLINE: 1 2 3 4 5 OVERALL DAY: 1 2 3 4 5

Am I closer to my goal today than I was yesterday?

☐ Yes   ☐ No

Final thought of the day:

_____

_____

_____

_____

_____

DAY 95

Date: _____

I am grateful for:

_____

_____

In 5 days, I will:

_____

_____

To achieve this, I will accomplish these three micro-goals today:

1. _____

2. _____

3. _____

My action plan for the day:

Task	Start Time	End Time
☐		
☐		
☐		
☐		
☐		

EVENING

Wonderful things that happened today:

_____

_____

_____

Three struggles I encountered:

1. _____

2. _____

3. _____

Possible solutions for these struggles:

1. _____

2. _____

3. _____

DISCIPLINE: 1 2 3 4 5   OVERALL DAY: 1 2 3 4 5

Am I closer to my goal today than I was yesterday?

☐ Yes   ☐ No

Final thought of the day:

_____

_____

_____

_____

_____

DAY 96

MORNING

I am grateful for:

_____

_____

In 4 days, I will:

_____

_____

To achieve this, I will accomplish these three micro-goals today:

1. _____

2. _____

3. _____

My action plan for the day:

Task	Start Time	End Time
☐		
☐		
☐		
☐		
☐		

EVENING

Wonderful things that happened today:

_____

_____

_____

Three struggles I encountered:

1. _____

2. _____

3. _____

Possible solutions for these struggles:

1. _____

2. _____

3. _____

DISCIPLINE: 1 2 3 4 5   OVERALL DAY: 1 2 3 4 5

Am I closer to my goal today than I was yesterday?

☐ Yes   ☐ No

Final thought of the day:

_____

_____

_____

_____

_____

DAY 97

MORNING

I am grateful for:

_____

_____

In 3 days, I will:

_____

_____

To achieve this, I will accomplish these three micro-goals today:

1. _____

2. _____

3. _____

My action plan for the day:

Task	Start Time	End Time
☐		
☐		
☐		
☐		
☐		

EVENING

Wonderful things that happened today:

_____

_____

_____

Three struggles I encountered:

1. _____

2. _____

3. _____

Possible solutions for these struggles:

1. _____

2. _____

3. _____

DISCIPLINE: 1 2 3 4 5   *OVERALL DAY:* 1 2 3 4 5

Am I closer to my goal today than I was yesterday?

☐ Yes   ☐ No

Final thought of the day:

_____

_____

_____

_____

_____

DAY 98

Date: _____

I am grateful for:

_____

_____

In 2 days, I will:

_____

_____

To achieve this, I will accomplish these three micro-goals today:

1. _____

2. _____

3. _____

My action plan for the day:

Task	Start Time	End Time
☐		
☐		
☐		
☐		
☐		

EVENING

Wonderful things that happened today:

_____

_____

_____

Three struggles I encountered:

1. _____

2. _____

3. _____

Possible solutions for these struggles:

1. _____

2. _____

3. _____

DISCIPLINE: 1 2 3 4 5   OVERALL DAY: 1 2 3 4 5

Am I closer to my goal today than I was yesterday?

☐ Yes   ☐ No

Final thought of the day:

_____

_____

_____

_____

_____

DAY 99

MORNING

I am grateful for:

_____

_____

In 1 day, I will:

_____

_____

To achieve this, I will accomplish these three micro-goals today:

1. _____

2. _____

3. _____

My action plan for the day:

Task	Start Time	End Time
☐		
☐		
☐		
☐		
☐		

EVENING

Wonderful things that happened today:

_____

_____

_____

Three struggles I encountered:

1. _____

2. _____

3. _____

Possible solutions for these struggles:

1. _____

2. _____

3. _____

DISCIPLINE: 1 2 3 4 5   OVERALL DAY: 1 2 3 4 5

Am I closer to my goal today than I was yesterday?

☐ Yes   ☐ No

Final thought of the day:

_____

_____

_____

_____

_____

DAY 100

Date: _____

MORNING

I am grateful for:

_____

_____

Today I will:

_____

_____

To achieve this, I will accomplish these three micro-goals today:

1. _____

2. _____

3. _____

My action plan for the day:

Task	Start Time	End Time
☐		
☐		
☐		
☐		
☐		

EVENING

Wonderful things that happened today:

_____

_____

_____

Three struggles I encountered:

1. _____

2. _____

3. _____

Possible solutions for these struggles:

1. _____

2. _____

3. _____

DISCIPLINE: 1 2 3 4 5   OVERALL DAY: 1 2 3 4 5

Am I closer to my goal today than I was yesterday?

☐ Yes   ☐ No

Final thought of the day:

_____

_____

_____

_____

_____

CONGRATULATIONS!

YOU MADE IT TO
DAY 100

REACHING MY GOAL

What did you enjoy about following a step-by-step process over the past 100 days?

_____

_____

_____

_____

_____

_____

_____

What are the best habits you established over the past 100 days?

_____

_____

_____

_____

_____

_____

_____

What was the most consistent struggle you faced over the course of the 100 days?

_____

_____

_____

_____

_____

_____

_____

What are you most proud of in regards to your 100-day journey?

_____

_____

_____

_____

_____

_____

_____

It's time to keep the momentum rolling! What's your next step?

_____

_____

_____

_____

_____

_____

_____

"TO BE WHAT WE ARE, AND TO BECOME
WHAT WE ARE CAPABLE OF BECOMING,
IS THE ONLY END OF LIFE."

—Robert Louis Stevenson

THOUGHTS, IDEAS, AND MUSINGS